C000143123

THE PAST IN PERSPECTIVE

*Series Editors: C.C. Eldridge and Ralph A. Griffiths*

# PROTESTANT DISSENTERS IN WALES, 1639–1689

# THE PAST IN PERSPECTIVE

*Series Editors: C.C. Eldridge and Ralph A. Griffiths*

*C.C. Eldridge* is Reader in History at St David's University
College, Lampeter, University of Wales.

*Ralph A. Griffiths* is Professor of Medieval History at University
College of Swansea, University of Wales.

Other titles in this series:

THE PAST IN PERSPECTIVE

# PROTESTANT DISSENTERS IN WALES, 1639–1689

*Geraint H. Jenkins*

CARDIFF
UNIVERSITY OF WALES PRESS
1992

© Geraint H. Jenkins, 1992


British Library Cataloguing-in-Publication Data.
A catalogue record for this book is available from
the British Library.

ISBN 0-7083-1140-7

Typeset at Alden Multimedia Ltd., Northampton
Printed in Great Britain by Billings Book Plan Ltd., Worcester

# Contents

*To my family*

# Editors' Foreword

Each volume in this series, *The Past in Perspective*, deals with a major theme of British, European or World history. The aim of the series is to engage the interest of all for whom knowledge of the riches of the world's historical experience is a delight, and in particular to meet the needs of students of history in universities and colleges — and at comparatively modest cost.

Each theme is tackled at sufficient length and in sufficient depth to allow each writer both to advance our understanding of the subject in the light of the most recent research, and to place his or her approach in due perspective. Accordingly, each volume contains a historiographical chapter which assesses how interpretations of its theme have developed, and have been criticized, endorsed, modified or discarded. Each volume, too, includes a section of substantial excerpts from key original sources: this reflects the importance of allowing the reader to come to his or her own conclusions about differing interpretations, and also the greater accessibility nowadays of original sources in print. Furthermore, in each volume there is a detailed bibliography which not only underpins the writer's own account and analysis, but also enables the reader to pursue the theme, or particular aspects of it, to even greater depth; the explosion of historical writing in the twentieth century makes such guidance invaluable. By these perspectives, taken together, each volume is an up-to-date, authoritative and substantial exploration of themes, ancient, medieval and modern, of British, European, American and World significance, after more than a century of the study and teaching of history.

C.C. Eldridge and Ralph A. Griffiths

*Explanatory note*

References in the course of the text to the Bibliography at the end of the book are indicated by a bold number in round brackets (**3**).

References to the Illustrative Documents which follow the main text are indicated by a bold roman numeral preceded by the word 'DOCUMENT', all within square brackets [**DOCUMENT XII**].

# Acknowledgements

I wish to express my sincere gratitude to the following: the British Academy for a generous grant which enabled me to undertake the necessary research; the staff of the Bodleian Library, Oxford, Dr Williams's Library, London, Friends House Library, London, the Glamorgan Record Office, Cardiff, the Gwynedd Archives Service, Caernarfon, the Hugh Owen Library, University College of Wales, Aberystwyth, and the National Library of Wales, Aberystwyth, for placing their records at my disposal; Professor R. Geraint Gruffydd, Mr B.G. Owens and Mr J. Glyn Parry for patiently answering my queries; the editors for their constructive advice; Mrs Carys Briddon for transforming my untidy manuscript into an immaculate type-script; Mrs Ceinwen Jones of the University of Wales Press for helpful guidance; and, last but not least, my wife and children for their forbearance.

Geraint H. Jenkins
October 1991

Mens faces, voices, differ much
saincts are not all one size
flowers in one garden vary too
lett none monopolize

Morgan Llwyd

# 1. 'Study in History, tis Pleasant, the Lord Make it Profitable'

Writing in the heyday of Dissent in mid-nineteenth century Wales, Evan Jones (better known as Ieuan Gwynedd), probably the most deeply loved Congregationalist minister of his time, readily acknowledged the heroic labours of early pioneers of Dissent in Stuart Wales:

> Welsh Nonconformity . . . was but the smoking flax at first; but at last the breath of persecution fanned it into a great flame, which has consumed, to a great extent, the moral wilderness of our native land. Many a bright name has been inscribed on the illustrious roll of its disciples. To Wales it has proved a 'burning and a shining light', and through its portals 'many sons' have entered the land of glory.

Early Dissenting records are scanty and diffuse, and many a 'bright name' might have been lost to us had not Edmund Calamy, the first serious historian of Dissent, published *An Account of the Ministers ... Ejected or Silenced after the Restoration in 1660* (2 vols., 1713), in which he chronicled the sufferings of ejected ministers and sought to repair the damage done to their reputation by the defamatory remarks of Anthony Wood and other Anglican apologists. (3) 'To let the Memory of these Men Dye is injurious to Posterity', wrote Calamy, and for our purposes it is fortunate that his material on Welsh Dissenters was provided by James Owen, a native of Carmarthenshire and the remarkably well-informed and talented tutor of the Dissenting academy at Oswestry. Calamy's work, however, provoked a storm of protest, largely because he had portrayed the established church as an engine of persecution. No one was more outraged than John Walker, rector of St Mary's Church, Exeter, and an unusually bilious Tory controversialist. In 1714 he published his celebrated riposte to Calamy — *An Attempt towards recovering an Account of the Numbers and Sufferings of the Clergy of the Church of England* — 700 pages which sought to reveal the manner in which clerics had been robbed of their livings and badly treated in the period 1642–59. (29) As far as Welsh evidence was concerned, most of the grist for Walker's mill was provided by the venomous anti-Propagation tracts of Alexander

Griffith, the arch-enemy of the Puritan cause in republican Wales. Walker's testimony was therefore riddled with half-truths, errors and disparaging remarks which bore witness to the obsessive hatred which so many high churchmen nursed towards Dissenters during the reign of Queen Anne.

The dust had barely settled following this furious skirmish when the Methodist movement emerged in the mid-1730s. The mouthpiece of the Methodist cause in Wales was William Williams, Pantycelyn, the supremely gifted hymnologist and prose writer. Williams believed that the evangelical movement had received the divine stamp of approval and that the labours of his Dissenting predecessors had been woefully inadequate. In his view, the 'Sun of Righteousness' had begun to spread its powerful rays over a dark and sleepy land from 1735 onwards. Wales had lain in 'a dark and deathly sleep' in pre-Methodist times, with 'neither presbyter, priest nor bishop astir' until the trumpet voice of Howel Harris and his colleagues had roused the natives from their spiritual torpor. (35) The reluctance of Methodist spokesmen to acknowledge their debt to their Anglican and Dissenting inheritance caused no small distress, and Edmund Jones, Congregationalist minister at Pontypool, angrily rebuked Williams Pantycelyn for his 'shameless untruth'. But, as far as Dissenters were concerned, the damage had been done. As the evangelical movement gathered pace, readers of sermons, prose works and periodicals were provided with a one-dimensional view of the past. Dissenters discovered that their objections were swamped by an extravagant flood of hagiography designed to ensure that the 'Methodist' view of history prevailed. In 1820 Robert Jones of Rhos-lan suffused his *Drych yr Amseroedd* (*A Mirror of the Times*, reprinted in 1841, 1888 and 1898) with 'the Apocrypha of the Revival' presented in the form of thumbnail sketches of saintly heroes and beguiling anecdotes of their sufferings and successes. (40) So influential was his work that by 1831 A.J. Johnes was moved to proclaim that 'the history of Dissent in Wales is the history of Methodism'. (38) The argument was clinched when a series of Methodist blockbusters successfully swept the history of pre-1735 Dissent into the margins of Welsh history. The most notable was John Hughes's *Methodistiaeth Cymru* (*Welsh Methodism*, 3 vols., 1851–6), a work of 1,828 pages which balefully concluded that pre-evangelical Wales had 'remained in a stygian black night — having sunk, to a pitiful extent, into ignorance, superstition and foolishness'. (36)

Even the fine Baptist historian, Joshua Thomas, was beguiled by the highly partisan view peddled by Methodist enthusiasts. A native of Carmarthenshire, Thomas served as Baptist minister of Etnam Street Church, Leominster, from 1753 to 1797. Over a period of thirty years he gathered valuable material on early Welsh Baptist initiatives, travelling widely on horseback to examine church registers, interview local sages and record stories and legends which would otherwise have been lost forever. By the standards of the age his *Hanes y Bedyddwyr Ymhlith y Cymry* (*History of the Baptists Among the Welsh*, 1778) was a conspicuously fair-minded and careful volume. (**27**) However, in his eagerness to upstage Congregationalists he argued on the basis of highly circumstantial evidence that the true mother church of Welsh Dissent was the Baptist church at Olchon, which he claimed had been established on the borders of Hereford-shire, Monmouthshire and Breconshire in 1633. Crucially, too, Thomas fell under the spell of Methodist historiography. His work was written at a time when the forces of evangelical revivalism were transforming Welsh Dissent and, although he extolled the heroic deeds of his forebears, he remained firmly convinced that 'a great revival' had occurred around 1735 and that the quality of spiritual life in Wales had subsequently changed in an extraordinary manner.

As the nineteenth century unfolded, Dissenters who were not Methodists became more numerous and also more acutely conscious of their historical roots. As they became more active in politics and in their campaign against the 'alien' established church, greater efforts were made to appeal to the past and rediscover the authentic Dissent-ing heritage. In particular, the Anti-State Church Association (founded in 1844 and later called the Liberation Society) perceived the past in the light of immediate religious and political objectives. As a result, early Puritan saints like John Penry, Walter Cradock and Vavasor Powell were venerated and the second centenary of the 'Great Ejection' of 1662 was publicly commemorated. In order to ensure that the early Dissenting fathers were suitably honoured, Dr Thomas Rees, Congregational minister at Swansea, published his remarkably influential *History of Protestant Nonconformity in Wales* (1861). Two thousand copies were swiftly sold and a second enlarged edition followed in 1883. (**24**) Unlike his predecessors, Rees had much more than a nodding acquaintance with manuscript material in public archives and he assembled a mass of information from Dissenting 'church books' which are no longer extant. But his work was marred by his avowed aim, expressed in the preface, to promote 'the cause of religion and religious liberty'. His fidelity to Dissent meant that he was reluctant to say anything which might tarnish the image of his forefathers. Indeed, he interpreted the beginnings of Dissent in such extravagantly heroic terms that even Methodists sniggered.

Such derision turned to anger in Methodist circles when it was alleged that Rees had deliberately tampered with official statistics in order to exaggerate the number of Dissenting conventiclers and the extent of their influence. In 1872 William Williams, author of *Welsh Calvinistic Methodism*, accused Rees of laundering statistics compiled by John Evans in order to inflate the importance of pre-Methodist Dissent. In their twin-volume filibuster, *Y Tadau Methodistaidd* (*The Methodist Fathers*, 1895–7), John Morgan Jones and William Morgan, both august Methodists, publicly claimed that Rees (who died in 1885) had deliberately misled, even cheated, his readers. In an extraordinary attempt to reassert the increasingly vulnerable 'Methodist' view of history, they insisted that the Welsh people had slept deeply in the arms of Morpheus before the 'great revival' of 1735 and that the sloth, formality and dryness of Dissent had proved major obstacles to the growth of true religion. (39) Dissenters were understandably outraged and more than eager to rise to the bait. The most notable riposte came from Beriah Gwynfe Evans, an opinionated Congregationalist who was better known in his day as a playwright and journalist than as a historian. In an iconoclastic work called *Diwygwyr Cymru* (*Welsh Revivalists*, 1900), Evans poured scorn on the 'self-appointed champions of Welsh Methodism', besmirched the character of Howel Harris, and belittled the achievements of eighteenth-century evangelicals. (34) Evans's father had forsaken the Calvinistic Methodists in unhappy circumstances and the memory of this tiff, together with his keenness to vindicate the work of Thomas Rees, prompted him to denigrate the Methodist movement. His work, it must be said, was intemperate and foolish. In spite of the copious footnotes and parade of learning on every page, it is clear, in fact, that Evans had failed to consult primary sources and neglected to check the reliability of secondary material. None the less, 20,000 copies of his book were sold and tongues wagged furiously throughout Wales.

A bitter debate, which served to bring out the worst in the warring factions, followed in the Nonconformist press. Both sides even traded insults in the columns of the *Western Mail*. No episode epitomizes more clearly the denominational bigotry which characterized historical writing in nineteenth-century Wales. As the sagging shelves of the National Library of Wales, not to mention second-hand bookshops, bear ample witness, much energy was expended by authors in debating the merits and demerits of Dissent and Methodism. On the whole, more heat than light was generated, primarily because both parties were committed advocates of a particular denominational position. It is, of course, the easiest thing in the world for the modern professional historian, surrounded by modern technology and all kinds of tools for research, to belittle the prodigious labours and deride the shortcomings of nineteenth-century historians of religion, but the fact remains that they were uncritical and often starry-eyed peddlers of hagiography.

The first Welsh historian to set himself the unenviable task of liberating the historiography of Welsh Dissent from the chains of hagiography was Dr Thomas Richards (1878–1962), the son of a Cardiganshire cottager, who taught history in schools from 1905 until 1926, when he was appointed librarian of the University College of North Wales, Bangor, a post which he held until 1946. Richards was greatly influenced by his mentor, Sir John Lloyd. He also struck up a friendship with Thomas Shankland, an extremely industrious but self-effacing bibliophile whose articles on pre-Methodist Wales in *Seren Gomer* (1900–4) not only genuinely broke new ground but also effectively demolished the reputation of Beriah Gwynfe Evans as a serious historian. (45) According to Richards, Shankland was a born researcher — 'he was a nose and an eye, a ear and a hand' — and it was he who persuaded him to embark on a programme of archival work on Puritanism and Dissent which was to prove much more durable and convincing than any previous work on religion in the seventeenth century. Both men were university graduates and there is no doubt that the setting up of the University of Wales in 1893 and the foundation of the National Library of Wales in 1907 were beginning to widen the gap between blinkered amateur enthusiasts and detached professional scholars. Despite heavy teaching commit-ments at school, Richards embarked on archival research which involved considerable financial sacrifices (he employed professional copyists in Oxford's Bodleian Library) and long hours of independent labour. He was determined to undertake rigorous research on a pro-fessional and objective basis, and he nursed a profound contempt for colleagues who exhibited a 'pronounced disinclination to walk up boldly to the doors of the public archives'. Shyness is not a trait one associates with Thomas Richards. He used to march into reading-rooms, pester custodians of public and private archives, and disarm them either with his engaging sense of humour or his encyclopaedic knowledge. During the 1920s he published six major works — an

aggregate total of 1,601 pages — which marked him out as the outstanding authority on Stuart Puritanism and Dissent in Wales. (**94,
97, 119, 120, 121, 122**) His works remain indispensable even today to
every serious student of the subject.

The major value of Richards's works is that they injected much-
needed intellectual and historical rigour into the debate about the
origins and nature of the Puritan inheritance. He sifted through and
analysed a mass of yellowing papers in the Public Record Office, the
Bodleian Library and Lambeth Palace Library, he thumbed the dusty
pages of printed tracts in the British Museum and the National
Library of Wales, and he acquired not only an unrivalled grasp of the
material but also a manifest devotion to the subject. His books are
replete with solid detail and profuse footnotes, the fruits of diligent
and fair-minded probing of sources. He possessed the detective's
delight in unravelling mysteries, chasing hares and exposing the
errors of colleagues. Although his forthright judgements on erring
historians sometimes caused offence, his aim was to ensure more
rigorous standards of scholarship and critical thought in academic
circles in Wales. It must be said, however, that readers with little
background knowledge coming to his books for the first time will find
them wellnigh indigestible. Not even Richards's most ardent admirer
would claim that his volumes make exciting reading. Indeed, his
works are riddled with convoluted sentences, extraordinary circum-
locutions, rhetorical questions, biblical allusions and baffling digressions. Often he would think aloud or debate with himself in the text.
Sometimes he would lose both himself and the reader in a welter of
subordinate clauses as he laboured to resolve what he called 'surmises'
or 'sidelights': 'straying a little', he used to confess with unrepentant
glee, 'but in a good cause.' As a result, the books which he wrote in
English never truly succeeded in conveying the sense of satisfaction
and pleasure which his communion with Puritans and Dissenters had
given him. Conversely, when lecturing or writing in Welsh, he could
be irresistibly eloquent and engaging. He was a marvellous raconteur
and his all-too-brief autobiographical excursions — *Atgofion Cardi*
and *Rhagor o Atgofion Cardi* (*Reminiscences of a Cardi* and *Further
Reminiscences of a Cardi*) — were written with unusual insight,
fluency and wit. A larger-than-life personality, 'Doc Tom' was a rare
figure the like of which we shall never see again.

It is a nice irony that Richards should have died in 1962 on the
occasion of the tercentenary of the 'Great Ejection', and it was during
that year that R. Tudur Jones and B.G. Owens emphatically endorsed

Richards's view by revealing in a seminal article published in *Y Cofiadur* that the overwhelming majority of Puritan ministers in Wales had vacated their livings before the implementation of the Act of Uniformity. In the same year, R. Tudur Jones published a major volume on English Congregationalism which whetted appetites for *Hanes Annibynwyr Cymru (History of Welsh Congregationalists*, 1966), the standard history of Congregationalism in Wales. (**127**) This beautifully written book became an instant classic and is unlikely ever to be superseded. Based on an enviably wide range of primary sources and a firm command of theological and literary material, it provided an authoritative account of the contribution of Congregationalism to the Puritan-Dissenting tradition. Five years later Jones published a finely written biography (in Welsh) of the combative evangelist Vavasor Powell. (**90**) Such major works have been accompanied by a steady flow of highly readable articles on Puritan theology, godliness and worship. In many ways, the writings of R. Tudur Jones are akin to those of Thomas Richards insofar as they represent the fruits of meticulous research, demonic energy, and a sympathetic but critical appraisal of the subject. Where they differ is in presentation. While three generations of readers have understandably balked at Richards's hideous literary style, the works of R. Tudur Jones bear the unmistakable stamp of a literary craftsman. He is quite simply the most prolific and important writer on religion in Stuart Wales.

The history of Welsh Baptists, too, has been admirably served by historians. Thomas Richards himself was a Baptist and contributed many weighty and influential articles to the denomination's historical journal of which he was editor for twenty-five years. But Richards possessed no great gift for synthesis and the strands were eventually brought together by T.M. Bassett in *The Welsh Baptists* (1977), a lucid work based on a thorough knowledge of primary sources and deep reflection. (**134**) By contrast, we still await a full-scale study of Welsh Quakerism. Among other relatively recent works which throw light on Dissent are *The Dissenters* (1978) by Michael R. Watts, an extremely valuable volume which provides an excellent summary of current scholarship and also locates the Welsh experience in a wider framework, (**57**) and the present author's *Literature, Religion and Society in Wales, 1660–1730* (1978) which evaluates the prodigious literary endeavours of Dissenters, traces lines of continuity between Dissent and Methodism, and portrays the so-called Methodist revival as an evolutionary rather than a revolutionary event. (**163**) The frequency with which the phrase 'The Great Awakening' reverberates in recent books and articles, however, suggests that the thesis does not command universal support and that the rehabilitation of Dissent is by no means complete.

All in all, considerable progress has been made in the twentieth century. Hundreds of specialist studies, admittedly of variable quality, have been published in historical and denominational journals. Tastes and fashions may have changed, but Philip Henry's dictum — 'Study in History, tis pleasant, the lord make it profitable' — evidently still fires the imagination. Yet there is much still to be done, for the subject continues to bristle with unanswered questions. The social and economic background of Dissenters has hardly been investigated and there is room in particular for much more rigorous analysis of probate material; the role of women in sectarian activities and the extent to which their involvement decisively improved their status cry out for study; links between the evangelical drive of the Puritan propagators and the location of conventicles in the Restoration period need to be discovered; and we still await a detailed study of the implementation of the Penal Code. This essay, therefore, is designed to give the reader a broad indication of the state of the art and to stimulate young researchers to illuminate some of the darker corners of Dissenting history in Stuart Wales.

# 2. 'Wales is a Poor Oppressed People and Despised Also'

In the eyes of affluent and well-educated Puritans living in south-east England, early Stuart Wales was a bleak, inaccessible, upland province, hardly more inviting than the desolate wilderness of America. In such a dark corner of the land, Puritan values were known to very few and endorsed by still fewer. Several formidable practical difficulties confronted Puritan crusaders who were prepared to venture into such unpromising territory. Apart from the daunting terrain and wretched communications, there was 'the foul language of Taphydom' to cope with. In the taverns and coffee-houses of London, jokes about the guttural patois and amusing accents of the Welsh were legion, as the humiliating adventures of Welsh 'Taffies' like 'Sheffery ap Morgan' bear ample witness. 'Men . . . laugh at them', wrote Richard Baxter of the Welsh, 'for their ill accented broken language.' Monoglot Welsh peasants were strongly attached to superstition, magic and witchcraft, and most of their leisure hours were spent in dance, drink and song. Their poverty and illiteracy meant that they had no inkling of the meaning of words like 'Arminianism' and 'Predestination', and it was not unusual even for the well-to-do to abuse clergymen who were known or reputed to be flagrant pluralists or idle sots. A yeoman of Pendeulwyn in Glamorgan publicly declared that he would 'rather heare an old wives tale then to heare anie church man preach, that the gaggling of a gander is as good, and that there is noe truthe in what they saye'. While it would be wrong to claim that the clergy were hopelessly ineffectual (if that were the case, how can one explain the dogged attachment of the Welsh to the established church in the 1650s?), the lack of a preaching tradition and adequate educational facilities conspired to obstruct the growth of Puritan convictions.

Furthermore, Puritans in England believed that Wales was a con-servative, pro-royalist backwater, a land, according to Oliver Cromwell, of 'seduced ignorant people' who were unable either to rise above their socio-economic plight or to avail themselves of the liberating effects of the Gospel. Towns were small and the pool of men of substance and 'the industrious sorts' — the traditional supporters of Puritanism — was woefully shallow. 'Wales is a poor oppressed people', declared William Erbery mournfully, 'and despised also.' Writing more in sorrow than in anger, Morgan Llwyd, too, feared that his countrymen were living 'in the sieve of frivolity, and in the bile of bitterness'.

In spite of these handicaps, however, Puritans began to grow in numbers and influence during the 1630s in the principal market towns along the Welsh borders, in trading centres in Glamorgan and Monmouthshire, and in mercantile communities in south Pembrokeshire. In north-east Wales lecturers like Oliver Thomas and Walter Cradock helped to turn Wrexham, the largest town in north Wales, into a 'factious' centre of unconventional ideas. Cradock — dubbed 'a bold ignorant young fellow' by Bishop William Murray of Llandaff — spent eleven months living in Wrexham in 1635–6 and succeeded in capturing the imagination of pious people in the town, none more so than Morgan Llwyd, a mere stripling of sixteen who had been dispatched from his native Ardudwy to school at Wrexham. Angered by Cradock's success in emptying alehouses, irate maltsters eventually persuaded local bigwigs to deprive Cradock of his curacy and to drive him out of the town. Even so, it says much for Cradock's gifts as a preacher and as a sower of separatist seeds that a hundred years later Dissenters and Methodists in north Wales were called 'Cradockites'. Cradock moved south and found refuge in Brampton Bryan, Herefordshire, the home of the godly Puritan magistrate Sir Robert Harley and his mercurial wife Brilliana. The Harleys prided themselves on their circle of Puritan friends and used their considerable wealth and patronage to promote the careers of godly ministers. Cradock's persuasive tongue helped to accelerate the spiritual conversion of Vavasor Powell, a Radnorshire-born schoolmaster who, once he was able to give Wales his undivided attention in the 1650s, became the most selfless and committed propagator of the Gospel in Wales.

When Archbishop William Laud, desperately anxious to re-create the beauty of holiness within churches, began to enforce what Puritans believed to be popish innovations, a few brave clergymen in Wales openly deplored his autocratic tactics. Among them was William Wroth, rector of the parish of Llanfaches in Monmouthshire since 1617, and a man who had disseminated Puritan views following a dramatic personal conversion in 1625–6. In 1635, on the initiative of Bishop William Murray (who was probably fearful of Laud's

wrath), Wroth and William Erbery, minister of St Mary's and St
John's in Cardiff, were cited in the Court of High Commission for
neglecting to read the Book of Sports and wear the surplice, and for
outdoor preaching. [**DOCUMENT I**] The case was adjourned until
1638, when Erbery resigned his living and Wroth conformed.
Memories of Laud and his 'Egyptian task-masters' were not
forgotten. Nathan Rogers, who was born in Llanfaches in 1639, was
brought up to remember the oppressive manner in which Laud had
employed the Courts of High Commission and Star Chamber — 'the
one stinging like an Adder, the other biting like a Serpent' — to bend
separatists to his will. But Laud was not Wroth's most immediate
enemy. In his powerful fiefdom at Raglan Castle, some ten miles from
Llanfaches, the fabulously wealthy Marquis of Worcester — the most
fervent of Catholics — was not only shielding Jesuit priests but also
(so rumour had it) stockpiling arms and gunpowder, and drilling a
'Welsh Popish Army' ready to die on behalf of the recusant cause.
Fear of resurgent Catholicism roused the most dire apprehensions
among Protestants and Puritans in Monmouthshire. Well-born
recusants were determined to ensure that the 'old faith' should remain
a living force, and since local governors were so preoccupied with
their own personal ambitions — as the persistence of vicious feuding
and the flouting of age-old tenurial rights bear witness — Catholicism
was allowed to prosper.

Even so, geographical considerations and the importance of trading
links probably counted more heavily in favour of Puritanism than the
animus against Laud and Catholicism. The impediment of mountain
ranges, large expanses of marsh and moorland, and poor roads did not
apply in the case of east Monmouthshire. It was the closest part of
Wales to London and, more significantly, to the city and port of
Bristol. The constant traffic of merchants, ministers and lecturers
between Llanfaches and Bristol — traditionally the metropolis of
south Wales — meant that a county like Monmouthshire was much
more receptive to outside influences than the sheltered parts of rural
north and west Wales. Puritanism spread along the trade routes in
south Wales and tended to prosper best among well-to-do middling
sorts.

By 1640 there were ten congregations of separatists in London, but
the poverty of church records means that no one can tell with absolute
certainty how many separatist or semi-separatist churches existed in
Wales by that time. Not surprisingly, given Laud's predilection
for silencing, fining and torturing religious deviants, early Welsh

separatists shrouded their activities in secrecy. One long-term con-
sequence of the lack of detailed evidence regarding the location and
activities of fugitive ensembles of separatists has been the enthusiasm
with which local patriots have subsequently claimed that the first
Congregationalist or Baptist churches were established in their own
particular communities. Charles Wilkins, historian of Merthyr Tydfil,
confidently declared that conventiclers secretly worshipped at
Blaencannaid farmhouse as early as 1620! But since Wilkins probably
drew on material assembled — or forged — by the impish Iolo
Morganwg, his claim is best discounted. (106) There is rather more
substance in Joshua Thomas's earnest claim that the first separatist
community was founded by Welsh Baptists in the isolated Olchon
valley, in the Welsh-speaking part of Herefordshire, in 1633.
Thomas's evidence, however, is largely circumstantial and his claim
was partly prompted by his devotion to his own denomination. It is
worth noting that he even believed that John Penry was a Baptist!
Having also read in Thomas Crosby's *History of the English Baptists*
(1738–40) that John Spilsbury had formed a separatist congregation
in London in September 1633, Thomas was anxious to ensure that
Welsh Baptists should not be seen to have tagged on the coat-tails of
their counterparts in England. We know that Baptists were recruiting
followers in the Olchon valley on the eve of the Civil War, but it is
hard to believe that a separatist assembly existed there as early as 1633.

Pride of place, therefore, as the seedbed of Welsh Protestant
Dissent must be given to the Congregationalist church of Llanfaches,
which is known to have been constituted in the last week of November
1639. Supported by his influential patron, Sir Edward Lewis of Y
Fan, near Caerphilly, William Wroth was the acknowledged head at
Llanfaches of a fledgeling community of gifted young preachers, each
of whom (with the single exception of Morgan Llwyd) hailed from the
border counties. Walter Cradock was a native of Trevela, near Usk in
Monmouthshire; Vavasor Powell was a freeholder's son from
Knucklas in Radnorshire; Richard Symonds came from a well-to-do
family in Abergavenny; Henry Walter was a Chepstow man; and
William Erbery was the son of a merchant from Roath-Dagfield in
Glamorgan. Wroth's wisdom and moderation elicited considerable
loyalty from his younger colleagues and it may have been on their
initiative that Henry Jessey, a Yorkshireman of Welsh descent who
was pastor of the Jacob circle of churches in London, was invited to
Llanfaches to advise and assist them as they embarked on a truly
historic course.

The gathered church established at Llanfaches in November 1639 was a voluntary body of like-minded men and women who bore witness against the liturgical innovations of Laud, separated themselves from the world, and dedicated their time, energy and spirit to serving Christ. The church was not overtly separatist or militant in its leanings. In accordance with the precepts of John Cotton, the Llanfaches saints adopted 'the New England way', which enabled members to enter into a binding Calvinist covenant without severing their links with the parish church. [**DOCUMENT II**] It is not clear how many rank-and-file members were familiar with Cotton's model, but they were evidently happy to continue worshipping in the parish church, endorse tithes, and permit those who favoured believers' baptism to join them. To some degree, therefore, they represented a godly community of saints whose worship supplemented rather than undermined the parochial system. Their admiration for Wroth as a preacher bordered on adulation and his fame as 'the Apostle of Wales' spread far beyond the boundaries of Monmouthshire. Dozens, possibly hundreds, of godly people from neighbouring counties on both sides of the Severn flocked to Llanfaches and, as William Erbery warmly recalled in later years, 'all was Spirit and life' under Wroth's ministry. Wroth, who liked to style himself 'preacher of God's word', went to great pains to satisfy the spiritual needs of enthusiastic pilgrims, even to the extent of preaching in the open air when the parish church was filled to overflowing.

As the foundations of Laudianism began to crumble in 1640–1, other groups of sectaries came into the open. At Wrexham Puritan yeomen and traders acquired a reputation for 'gadding to sermons', while William Erbery's conventicle at Cardiff was fervently anticlerical. At Ambrose Mostyn's church in Swansea, pious middling sorts listened astutely to Puritan sermons and bestowed scriptural Christian names on their children, while well-to-do burgesses at Haverfordwest actively promoted the principles of separation. In the mean time, strenuous efforts were made by leading Welsh Puritans to awaken Parliament to its spiritual responsibilities towards barren corners like Wales. Fear of foreign invasion and internal insurrection preyed on their minds, especially since they were convinced that the commitment of Charles I to Protestantism was so slender that he could no longer be trusted. Anti-popish sentiments prompted them to call for a speedy and vigorous programme of reformation. In June 1641 Walter Cradock eloquently urged members of the House of Commons to send godly preachers into Wales to save souls. Such

pleas became even more impassioned following the slaughter of
Protestants during the Catholic uprising in Ireland in the autumn.

Before separatist gains in Wales could be consolidated, the parliamentary challenge to the authority of the King ushered in civil war
in the summer of 1642. William Wroth had already died in 1641 and
was buried under either the threshold or the chancel of Llanfaches
Church, and his young disciples did not find it easy to organize and
maintain gathered churches in a land where royalist sentiment ran
strong. In parts of Breconshire Vavasor Powell was so cruelly abused
and manhandled by anti-Puritan zealots that he was glad to find
refuge in London. Walter Cradock's flock at Llanfaches were also
compelled to seek sanctuary among their Congregationalist colleagues
at the Broadmead Church in Bristol, where regular meetings were
held at an inn and a bakery. In July 1643, however, Bristol fell to the
royalists and Walter Cradock literally escaped from the city under the
noses of Princes Maurice and Rupert. Accompanied by the rump of
the Llanfaches congregation, Cradock settled in London and joined
the church of All Hallows the Great in Thames Street. These were
testing times for Welsh Puritans and Morgan Llwyd voiced their
anxieties when he spoke of the 'desolation of the Welsh Saints'.

Meanwhile, the struggle for power got under way on the battlefield,
and Roundhead zealots, encouraged by Parliament, began to
desecrate churches as well as shed blood. When Sir Thomas
Myddelton's troops crossed the River Dee into Wales in 1643, 'super-
stitious' images such as brasses, fonts, stained-glass windows and
organs in churches were pulled down [**DOCUMENT III**], while parliamentary armies in the south-east burned the records and library of
Llandaff Cathedral on the green of Cardiff Castle. Parliament, too, set
about dismantling Laudian 'innovations' and replacing them with a
Presbyterian polity. The Assembly of Divines, which met at Westminster from July 1643, was much exercised by matters of church
government and three years elapsed before the House of Commons
endorsed its recommendation that a Presbyterian model of church
government be established throughout England and Wales. It was
ordered that the Prayer Book be supplanted by a new Directory of
Worship, which was to be placed in every parish church throughout
Wales. As the Westminster Assembly deliberated over the question of
church government, Parliament entrusted the task of ejecting unsatis-
factory clergymen and replacing them with godly ministers to the
Committee for Plundered Ministers. In practice, however, these
schemes promised rather more than they delivered. Little effort was

made to establish properly constituted Presbyterian classes in Wales, much to the relief of supporters of the Prayer Book and even more to that of radical Congregationalists who believed that Presbyterianism was 'a limb of Antichrist'. Rigid, middle-class Presbyterianism did not commend itself to the disciples of William Wroth, who increasingly endorsed the independence of individual congregations and pressed for religious toleration and godly reformation. Nor were they happy with many of the appointments made to livings in Wales by the Committee for Plundered Ministers, the House of Commons and the House of Lords. By no means all the 130 ministers appointed to serve in Wales between 1644 and 1649 could properly be dubbed 'godly and painful'. Many were shameless opportunists, appointed on the recommendation of local committees, and complaints of nepotism and misconduct were legion. The purge of ungodly ministers proved such a haphazard process that calls for more speedy and effective measures of propagating the Gospel became more and more clamant. The enthusiasm of the Welsh clergy for the royalist cause exasperated radical sectarians who longed for the removal of 'dumb dogs' who neglected their flocks, visited alehouses and condoned Sunday sports. Soldiers and chaplains who had gone to war in order to rid the Welsh of a tyrannical monarch and enable Everyman to give an account of the divine Spirit within him called for much bolder initiatives. Walter Cradock unflinchingly advocated the cause of liberty of conscience, claiming that 'mechanic sorts' had every right to preach the glad tidings of the Gospel to the common man. [**DOCUMENT IV**] 'Every servant must exercise his talent', declared Morgan Llwyd.

Religious radicalism of this kind also drew strength from millenarian ideas which had been an intrinsic part of Protestant thinking since Elizabethan times. The turmoil of civil war, the abolition of episcopal government, the collapse of censorship and the proliferation of Bibles, sermons and pamphlets all helped to sharpen millennial expectations appreciably. Ardent Fifth Monarchists like Morgan Llwyd [**DOCUMENT V**] and Vavasor Powell were so deeply involved in the eschatological speculation of the times that they were convinced that the prophecies which foretold the collapse of four world-empires and the return of the Messiah to govern on earth with his chosen saints for a thousand years were about to be fulfilled. 'The pillars of the world are shaking', wrote Llwyd, 'and fire and tempest rage in every land round about.' A great sense of urgency and excitement prevailed as millenarians went to extraordinary lengths to decode scriptural passages which might help them forecast the precise year in

which 'King Jesus' would appear on earth and rule in harmony, peace
and prosperity with his favoured saints. They were absolutely certain
they were witnessing events whose consequences would prove long-
lasting. Within his own lifetime, Morgan Llwyd expected the fulfilment of divine promises:

> fifty goes big, or fifty sixe
> or sixty five some say
> But within mans age, hope to see
> all old things flung away.

In such a charged atmosphere, it was natural for radical sectarians
to argue that modest pruning of the clerical system was inadequate
and that much more vigorous chopping was required. In Thomas
Richards's words: 'There was nothing for it but to take the fan in
one's hand, thoroughly purge the threshing floor, and burn up the
chaff with unquenchable fire.' But the rigid and intolerant Presbyterians who held sway in Parliament displayed little or no enthusiasm
for the task of ejecting time-servers, pluralists and opportunists and
replacing them with pious, preaching ministers with fire in their
bellies. The problem remained unsolved until the royalist military
forces were finally torn to pieces by superior parliamentary strength
by the summer of 1648. Thereafter events moved swiftly. In
December Col. Thomas Pride sent conservative members of the Long
Parliament packing, thereby clearing the way for more radical initiatives. The purged Commons was ordered by the army to set up a
special High Court of Justice, and a minority of determined Puritan
saints (among them the doughty colonel, John Jones of Maesygarnedd, Ardudwy) ensured that Charles I went to the block on 30
January 1649. A thrill of horror spread through Wales when news of
this never-to-be-forgotten deed was received. But ardent millenarians
were totally at ease with their consciences; they were convinced that
Charles was the embodiment of Antichrist and that his demise was a
clear sign of the Divine Will. Morgan Llwyd described Charles I 'as
the Last King of Britain', and by 1650 he and Vavasor Powell were
busily assembling durable pockets of supporters on the Welsh borders
and preparing for a powerful programme of evangelization which
would not only save the souls of their benighted countrymen but also
help to hasten the second coming of the Saviour.

# 3.   'The Purgation of the Temple'

Mindful of the considerable political advantages involved, the Rump Parliament eventually bowed to the demands of a highly influential core of zealous Puritan preachers and military commanders — led by the radical Cornish firebrand Hugh Peter — who had sedulously pressed the case for full-scale evangelization in Wales. The pace of reform accelerated sharply when, on 22 February 1650, the Act for the Better Propagation and Preaching of the Gospel in Wales was passed. This statute constituted the most seminal piece of legislation in the history of religion in Wales since the act of 1563 which had required the bishops of Wales and Hereford to provide a Welsh translation of the Bible and Prayer Book. With pardonable exaggeration, Dr Thomas Richards once described the act of 1650 as 'the nearest thing Wales ever acquired to Home Rule'!

The Propagation Act enabled the state to seize church assets and use them to finance large-scale evangelization by means of preaching ministers and primary education. Seventy-one Commissioners, headed by Col. Thomas Harrison, a fervent Fifth Monarchist, were appointed and given authority to eject inadequate clergymen and set aside a fifth of the value of a living for the upkeep of their wives and children. The Commissioners were also empowered to resolve indemnity disputes and reallocate tithe payments. In practice, however, such powers were exercised by powerful juntas of military men and radical squires who assembled regularly in the larger market towns of Wales and placed allegedly delinquent ministers under strict scrutiny. Over a period of three years a total of 278 clergymen (including 196 from south Wales) — 'idle and self-feeding shepherds', as Vavasor Powell called them — failed to pass muster and were deprived of their livings. A second body of twenty-five Approvers, each of whom was a well-regarded and pious Puritan, was given the more challenging task of recruiting and appointing suitably qualified preachers and schoolmasters to fill the vacancies occasioned by what John Lewis, Glas-crug, called 'the purgation of the Temple'.

No stone was left unturned in a bid to attract gifted and energetic preachers, and eventually the recruiting drive realized seventy-five English-speaking ministers, sixty Welsh-speaking ministers and sixty-three itinerant ministers, the overwhelming majority of whom served the needs of citizens in south Wales and the borders.

Opponents of propagation lost no time in condemning the scheme. Indeed, the implementation of the act provoked an explosion of hostile criticism. The orchestrator of this campaign was Alexander Griffith, a malevolent cleric whose ejection from the livings of Glasbury and Llanwnnog in Radnorshire in June 1650 on account of alleged drunkenness and lasciviousness had left him with an acute sense of grievance. Griffith's pamphlets, notably the celebrated *Strena Vavasoriensis* (1654), were an unsubtle admixture of truths, half-truths and untruths. [**DOCUMENT VI**] He was not above bes-mirching the character and qualifications of so-called tinkers, tailors and thatchers who staffed the itinerant ranks or of portraying the leading saints and administrators as get-rich-quick adventurers. In particular, he reserved special strictures for his *bête noire*, Vavasor Powell, and cruelly misrepresented him as a grievous hypocrite, peculator and oppressor. Anti-propagation petitions, sponsored by gentlemen and clergymen with axes to grind, also kept the printing presses busy. Tales of Col. John Jones's forthright statements, the brusque behaviour of Hugh Peter and much sword-waving by Vavasor Powell strengthened people's conviction that the Propaga-tion Act was essentially a military exercise implemented by Saxon soldiers, bureaucrats and sequestrators.

It is undoubtedly the case that, over a period of three years, intensive and sometimes none too scrupulous efforts were made to preach the Gospel and to introduce what Puritans considered the civilizing benefits of English law, administration and culture to one of the proverbially barren corners of the land. No one should deny the idealism and the determination of the Puritan saints as they vigor-ously pursued their dream of building a New Jerusalem. The central figure in the campaign was Vavasor Powell; always controversial, he remained almost continuously in the public eye on account of his zealous preaching and his sometimes ruthless advocacy of the Puritan faith. With invincible optimism, Powell led the way. He was a preacher of prodigious energy who threw himself into the task of spreading the Puritan gospel in the border counties with zeal and commitment the like of which, he claimed, had never been wit-nessed since the days of the Apostles. [**DOCUMENT VII**] Those who campaigned with him were inspired and sustained by his enthusiasm. Rousing sermons were delivered in parish churches, churchyards, market squares and private homes. In the north-east Ambrose Mostyn embarked on exhausting preaching missions, while Morgan Llwyd, who was based in Wrexham, even ventured to the fastnesses of the Llŷn peninsula, where he caused a stir by brandishing his Bible and preaching loudly in Pwllheli market. Walter Cradock, too, displayed his skills in 'speaking to men's very hearts' in his beloved Usk valley, where he seized every opportunity to proclaim the grace of God to wretched sinners.

Another significant and forward-looking feature of the Propagation Act was the grant afforded by the state to establish a rudimentary system of elementary education. In a bid to banish 'ignorance and profaneness' among the young, sixty-three schools were established in the major market towns and were designed to introduce sons and daughters of Puritan middling sorts to the 'three Rs' through the medium of the English language. This was the first occasion on which the state had made any kind of provision for education in Wales and the scheme itself subsequently became a prototype for privately funded charity schools.

Those who led and contributed to this powerful missionary campaign were convinced that their unstinting labours had a profound effect upon spiritual life in Wales. Oliver Cromwell declared that it was a glorious and honourable experiment, and even Richard Baxter, who seldom lost an opportunity to stigmatize itinerant preachers, conceded that 'serious godliness encreased'. Vavasor Powell vigorously maintained until his dying day that the Propagation Act was a major success story. He spoke fondly of the hundreds of members who attended cells of Christian piety and who walked proudly 'in love and fear of the Lord'. The Propagation undoubtedly proved a shot in the arm for the Congregational cause in Wales, for the Approvers, true to the ideals of John Penry and William Wroth, favoured those 'visible saints' who believed in autonomous local churches, liberty of conscience and godly discipline.

In spite of these impassioned claims, the plain truth is that the propagators failed to honour their promises and fulfil their ambitions. This was partly, of course, because the House of Commons obstructed further progress by refusing to renew the act on 1 April 1653. But long before then, for those with eyes to see, there were glaring weaknesses and anomalies in the implementation of the mission. It had proved immeasurably easier to rob allegedly unfit clergy of their livings than

to discover pious Puritans to fill their places. University graduates
were reluctant to venture into penurious, Welsh-speaking Wales, and
by recruiting itinerant preachers the propagators not only admitted
failure but also employed men who were not, at least in the conven-
tional sense, qualified to preach. It was widely, and probably legitimately, claimed that countless parishes suffered neglect because even
the most energetic itinerants were unable to cope. Although we
should beware of placing too much faith in Anglican caricatures of
'base-born' itinerants, Welsh-speaking communities could scarcely
have warmed to newcomers bearing names like Fogg, Glendale, Ible,
Rushworth and Townesend. Nor were the traditional rulers of society
happy to discover that the propagators had turned their world upside
down. Irreverent and subversive sermons preached by 'lay ignor-
amuses and schismatics' horrified gentlemen and clergymen alike. In
their minds, fear of the authority of the sword was matched by fear of
social revolution.

The fearful sense of desolation and gloom which afflicted fervent
churchmen is best conveyed in the literature of the times. It is a
strange irony, in fact, that the painful and humiliating years of propagation should have provoked a burst of marvellously creative writing
by champions of the established church. Huw Morys, Henry
Vaughan, Rowland Vaughan, Rowland Watkyns and Jeremy Taylor
were all inspired to keep the flame of Anglicanism burning. There was
strong sympathy in Wales for the ejected clergy and many of them
continued to conduct Anglican services according to the traditional
liturgy in private homes. But many of them were in dire economic
straits and extremely bitter. In plaintive verse and prose, Henry
Vaughan, the self-styled Silurist, movingly expressed the deep sense
of humiliation and anguish felt not only by fellow clergymen but also
by 'captive' fellow countrymen. [**DOCUMENT VIII**] Vaughan's
contemplations were deeply coloured by Puritan violence against
respected clerics, the spilling of blood on battlefields and the beheading
of the King. He despised those 'barbarous persons without light or perfection' who had risen in army ranks and civilian posts, usurped holy
offices, and proved utterly subversive of rank, degree and convention.

The missionary drive was also badly affected by adverse publicity
regarding the actual day-to-day administration of the act. During the
years of propagation, and for many afterwards, Wales was awash with
rumours of peculation and cupidity, and unsubstantiated tales of land
deals, arbitrary confiscations, tithe appropriation and shameless corruption. It was widely believed that the Propagation Commission was

staffed by cynical adventurers who used the mission as a cloak for their own selfish ambitions. In south Wales, particularly Glamorgan, Puritan propagation and profiteering often went hand in hand. Well-affected middling sorts and tithe farmers not only welcomed the substantial measure of decentralization which propagation entailed but also the undoubted material benefits. The wealth and influence of some Commissioners was clearly an embarrassment to saintly Puritans and administrators of integrity. Most hostile fingers were pointed at Col. Philip Jones, 'the uncrowned King of south Wales'. Jones was a freeholder from Llangyfelach whose meteoric rise to power as a soldier (his family crest bore a mailed fist holding a spear) and an administrator had enabled him to acquire extensive property and no small influence in the corridors of power at Westminster. Even his supporters were at a loss to explain his extraordinarily rapid advancement and riches, and his upward mobility seemed to personify the tawdry acquisitiveness which characterized Puritan rule in republican Wales. Jones, however, strenuously denied all the charges made against him and somehow managed to cover his tracks wonderfully well. Having superintended Oliver Cromwell's funeral and burial in September 1658, he quietly retired from public life to his substantial estate at Fonmon Castle in the Vale of Glamorgan, and duly made his peace with the royalist regime in 1660. In mid-Wales, Vavasor Powell was accused by his arch-enemy Alexander Griffith of double standards, cupidity and maladministration. Powell vigorously pleaded his innocence and his disciples immediately sprang to his defence, but the damage done to his reputation was beyond repair. In north Wales disreputable military careerists like Col. John Carter and Col. George Twisleton let few opportunities of acquiring handsome offices and broad acres slip from their grasp, and their behaviour made a mockery of the notion that propagation was an honourable mission governed by honest saints. Even Morgan Llwyd glumly confessed that some 'unruly birds' plundered willy-nilly. Although no one ever succeeded in proving that the propagators were cooking the books, suspicions lingered on for a very long time. Even as late as 1714 John Walker's celebrated account of sufferings under the Propagation Act contained many dark hints of dishonesty and corruption.

Controversy over the validity of state-subsidized Puritanism and the matter of tithes also made life difficult for the propagators. Several saints had grave misgivings about receiving maintenance from the public purse. None wrestled more furiously with his conscience than William Erbery, the prickliest of Puritans, and eventually in 1652 he denounced tithes as a Jewish burden and refused to accept a salary for his work as a propagator. [**DOCUMENT IX**] It was fashionable at the time, notably in learned circles, to claim that Erbery delighted in perversity for its own sake and that his 'disease lay in his Head, not in his Heart'. Such a condescending view does Erbery an injustice. He was certainly a complex, argumentative figure, but he was deeply versed in the politics of the day and his sermons reflect a genuinely moving moral sense of justice. A popular champion of the common man, he had served as a chaplain in the New Model Army, immersed himself in the writings of Thomas Brightman, Jacob Boehme and John Saltmarsh, and taken part in public discussions in London on the content of the famous Leveller manifesto, *The Agreement of the People*. During the propagation years Erbery not only published a flow of polemical tracts but also preached regularly in south-east Wales where his concern for the welfare of the 'Freeborn Welshman' among the deprived urban poor in towns like Newport, Cardiff and Bridgend and his barbed comments about wealthy monopolists and tithe-grabbing ministers aroused acute alarm in propertied circles. His experiences under Puritan godly rule taught him a good deal about greed and hypocrisy as well as about the iniquity of tithes and the legal system. In 1652 he wrote to Cromwell, urging him to ease the burdens of 'my dear Country-men in Wales' by 'raising a publique stocke out of the estates of the unrighteous rich ones, or parliamentary delinquents, and from the ruines of most unjust courts, judicatures, and judges'. Such radicalism was bound not only to offend traditional landowners but also to arouse the opposition of Puritan Commissioners whose voracious needs Erbery so loudly despised.

For all these reasons, the Act for the Propagation of the Gospel in Wales was implemented in an atmosphere of bitterness and recrimination. The act expired at the end of March 1653 and, outside Puritan circles, few tears were shed in Wales following its abrupt demise. Even so, it is hard to understand why such a potentially fruitful campaign should have been abandoned so summarily by the Rump Parliament. In retrospect, it could be argued that winding up the experiment, whatever its defects, was a colossal blunder. First of all, it led to the adoption of a more centralized approach. Devolution was abandoned and on 20 March 1654 power was vested in a London-based committee of thirty-eight distinguished Puritan divines. The Committee for the Approbation of Publicque Preachers (popularly known as the Triers) was given the task of reviewing previous

appointments and passing judgement on the qualifications of candidates who wished to be presented to settled livings. The aim was to
establish some kind of permanent national church, and following the
upheavals and uncertainties of the propagation period that ambition
was entirely understandable. Many excellent appointments were
made, among them Stephen Hughes (Meidrim), William Jones
(Cilmaenllwyd), Morgan Llwyd (Wrexham), Marmaduke Matthews
(Swansea) and Henry Walter (Newport), but the Triers, too, were
dogged by a chronic dearth of qualified ministers. Vetting candidates
was not always easy and the committee's insistence that no new
nominee could enter a living without a testimony signed by at least
three reputable persons (including a settled minister) meant that it
was rather too easily hoodwinked by witnesses who were economical
with the truth. In some of the remoter western counties of Wales the
work of the Triers was an abysmal failure. In faraway Anglesey, for
instance, livings were awarded to shameless opportunists and time-
servers simply because the Triers lacked local knowledge. Moreover,
the shortage of willing hands in the harvest field meant that the old
itinerant procedure was not entirely set aside, and John Lewis, Glas-
crug, was so concerned about the slow rate of recruitment that he
recommended reinstating clergymen who, in his view, had been
wrongly robbed of their livings by over-zealous propagators. Lewis
also entered into correspondence with Richard Baxter and Dr John
Ellis of Dolgellau regarding the possibility of establishing a Welsh
college in order to create a regular supply of well-trained, Welsh-
speaking ministers. (169) Nothing came of the scheme, however, and
such plans were buried until Victorian times. As far as the experiment
of the Triers is concerned, it is difficult not to believe that the cautious
middle course which they steered from their distant headquarters in
London served to let slip the opportunity to consolidate and strengthen the far more fundamental changes on which the propagators
had embarked.

Secondly, the Rump's refusal to extend the Propagation Commission's term of office ushered in disastrous splits in the ranks of leading
Welsh Puritans. Militant firebrands within the Fifth Monarchist
movement began to urge Cromwell to set up a godly Sanhedrin
designed to remove every impediment which might postpone the
arrival of King Jesus, and there was general rejoicing in their ranks
when the Rump Parliament was forcibly dissolved on 20 April 1653.
Gathered churches in Radnorshire warmly congratulated Cromwell
on his prescience and Vavasor Powell fervently expected that hence-

forth 'law should streame down like a river freely'. One hundred and fifty-three Fifth Monarchists in Denbighshire, many of them small traders, freeholders and craftsmen, penned their names to an address pleading with Cromwell to assemble a Parliament of saints and recommending the names of fit members. But when Cromwell finally bowed to the wishes of the millennialists, local congregations were not consulted and the six Welsh representatives who took their places in the newly constituted Nominated Parliament (commonly known as Barebone's Parliament) on 4 July 1653 were chosen on the recommendation of Major-General Thomas Harrison and Vavasor Powell. In a moving opening speech, Cromwell voiced his millennial aspirations and wished the saints well in their deliberations on behalf of 'the people of God'.

Messianic hopes were at their peak at this time, and Morgan Llwyd and Vavasor Powell were as one in their conviction that the fourth kingdom of Rome was approaching its nemesis and that Christ would shortly establish his fifth and final monarchy. In particular, the publication of Llwyd's *Gwaedd ynghymru yn wyneb pob Cydwybod* (*A Cry in Wales in the face of every Conscience*) and *Llyfr y Tri Aderyn* (*The Book of the Three Birds*) in the summer of 1653 helped to quicken the pulses of those who aspired to be God's chosen people. *Llyfr y Tri Aderyn*, Llwyd's most celebrated work, was a sharply etched political and religious allegory in which three principal characters, the Eagle (Oliver Cromwell), the Raven (the episcopal church) and the Dove (the Puritan saints), engaged in dialogue whose major purpose was to awaken the Welsh to their responsibility of preparing themselves for Christ's return and 'the summer of the faithful'. [**DOCUMENT X**] The Fifth Monarchist message, based on a shrewd mixture of genuine passion, excessive rhetoric and self-interest, was particularly attractive to traders, shopkeepers and artisans in the border towns, for it called for the abolition of tithes, customs, excise, monopolies and tyranny of all kinds. Many who had previously suspected that Puritanism was an alien plant were impressed not only by Llwyd's promise of a kingdom in which toleration, peace and prosperity would prevail but also by his manifest devotion to his country. Indeed, no reader of Llwyd's works can fail to be struck by his genuine love for 'tender hearted Britons'.

Although the assembled saints in Barebone's Parliament set about their tasks with Puritan-like zeal and application, rifts swiftly emerged between moderate Puritans and radical millenarian saints. Contentious issues such as the abolition of tithes and the reform of the law drove them apart, and it was no surprise when the experiment foundered in December 1653. Convinced that only he could avert the drift to anarchy, Cromwell accepted the position of Lord Protector, a deed which Fifth Monarchists regarded as a betrayal worthy of Judas Iscariot. In Vavasor Powell's eyes, Cromwell was an apostate, a blasphemer and usurper. He made no bones about his disapproval of the Lord Protector's actions, publicly denouncing him as 'the dissembleingst perjured villaine in the world'. A brief spell in prison failed to soothe Powell's animus against Cromwell. He travelled from London to Wales and continued to rant and rage against 'the little horn' (that is, Cromwell, the enemy of the saints) in incendiary sermons delivered in the border counties. Although Powell's flamboyant gestures and threats of vengeance (he once boastfully claimed that 20,000 Welsh saints awaited his call to arms) were not supported by actual rebellion, Cromwell's spies took no chances and kept him under close surveillance. Major-General James Berry invited him to discuss his grievances privately and advised him to act more prudently. Powell coolly protested his innocence and Berry took him at his word, wrongly as it turned out, for Powell's was a voice which could not be silenced. Indeed, he was determined to capture the headlines once more.

In December 1655 Richard Price of Gunley, one of Vavasor Powell's most loyal followers, delivered personally to Oliver Cromwell a sensational pamphlet entitled *A Word for God*. [DOCUMENT XI] It was a damning indictment by Powell of Cromwellian rule. Among other things, the Lord Protector was accused of apostasy and betrayal, deriding and incarcerating saints, imposing swingeing taxes, and condoning corruption in high places. The petition was signed by 322 ardent millenarians, most of whom were industrious middling sorts for whom the impending return of Jesus was something more than just a pious dream. Morale among Powell's old comrades in arms was low and Puritans who did not share his millennial convictions were convinced that his sole object was self-glorification. Walter Cradock immediately showed his colours by publishing a loyal counter-petition — *The Humble Representation and Address to his Highness of Several Churches and Christians in South Wales* (1656) — which was endorsed by 762 signatures. In fulsome terms, Cradock commended the Lord Protector's valiant efforts to keep the saints' republican ship afloat and deplored the traitorous deeds of saboteurs like Powell.

This flurry of petitioning was a clear sign of the stresses and strains which were dividing Puritan saints in Wales. More than any other of his contemporaries, Powell stood for the spirit of rebellion and he doggedly refused to admit that the millenarian cause was bankrupt. Although he was not without courage, Walter Cradock was a healer rather than a warrior. He had always remained unshakeably loyal to Cromwell. In an effusive letter written in March 1652, he revealed how he habitually prayed for Cromwell 'in a ditch, wood, or under a hey-mow', and when his hero died in September 1658 Cradock was one of the chosen few who attended the funeral. Cradock liked to keep a much lower profile than Powell. He was more cautious and balanced in his judgements, more tolerant towards others, and more anxious to build alliances. Puritan opinion in south Wales was solidly on his side and Powell was therefore condemned to impotent strife and discord on the Welsh borders.

Powell's intemperate behaviour also provoked a radical conflict of ideals and interests between himself and his colleague Morgan Llwyd. Powell had had the temerity to append Llwyd's signature to *A Word for God* without his permission and, although Llwyd was disappointed by Cromwell's apostasy in December 1653, he believed that the Protectorate deserved support, at least for the time being, lest a royalist revival encourage further turmoil and bloodshed. He turned his back on political agitation and took refuge in contemplation. 'Is this the Doore out of Babilon?' he wrote, 'or do ye knocke at a wrong gate? . . . Lett us . . . without private mutterings find our work and waite within ourselves on God.' Powell dubbed Llwyd a traitor and the two men went their separate ways. The differences between them were clearly rooted in character and temperament. Patience and discretion were not among Powell's virtues. A stubborn man, he never allowed expediency to sully his principles. Courageous to the point of recklessness, he possessed a fierce, ruthless streak which blinded him to the possibilities of united political action. Llwyd, for his part, had become disenchanted with political nostrums and was prone to lapse into intense bouts of self-scrutiny. Cradock's initial guidance, the experiences of bloody civil strife and the millennial cause had helped to mould Llwyd's thinking up until 1651, but from then onwards the mystical and contemplative ideas of the Continental spiritualist, Jacob Boehme, became the major influence on his life. Thirty-two separate English translations of Boehme's works were published between 1644 and 1662 and his thesis of the divine immanence within all objects deeply coloured many of Llwyd's poems and allegories. Even in *Llyfr y Tri Aderyn*, Llwyd had spoken not only of the literal return of

Christ but also of the inner millennium which had preoccupied Boehme. He believed that the true key to eternal happiness lay in the heart — 'Life lies in the spirit not in the letter' — and he became deeply suspicious of men's faith in outward forms and constitutions.

Llwyd became so deeply immersed in Boehmenism that his commitment to the millennial cause was bound to dwindle. He was happy to retire to the wings and leave Powell to occupy centre stage. His subsequent fame, therefore, rests principally on his talent as a writer. Between 1653 and 1657 he published eight works in Welsh and three in English which offered readers not only an exploration of the spiritual experiences which lay at the heart of Puritanism but also a rich variety of intellectual ideas and political dialectic. (101) These were remarkably productive years for Llwyd and his works deserve to be better known outside Wales. He was a conscious stylist who deployed his rich native cultural inheritance with extraordinary vividness. He experimented in the field of metaphysics and human psychology in the most subtle manner, and sought to celebrate the Holy Spirit by evolving new forms of rhetorical and poetical devices. Some of his work, it must be said, is dauntingly allusive, and even incomprehensible to the modern mind. One can well understand why his friend, Col. John Jones, Maesygarnedd, urged him to write in a plain, unvarnished style. But even Llwyd's most complex works were written with unfailing grace and distinction and they must be counted among the most extraordinary products of the Puritan Revolution in Wales. Indeed, it could be said of Morgan Llwyd, as it was once said of George Fox, that he was 'an original, being no man's copy'.

Nevertheless, personal disagreements, dog-fights and conflicts of priorities did not help the Puritans to present a united front in the face of their enemies or to deal effectively with the challenges posed by the Restoration in 1660. Indeed, by the time of Cromwell's death in 1658 the Puritan movement in Wales was hopelessly fragmented. This was the inescapable result of the failure of the Rump Parliament to give a further vote of confidence to the Propagators. Robbed of a common cause, the Welsh saints drifted apart and were never again able to stimulate a genuine spiritual revolution. The leading evangelists burned themselves out. William Erbery had died, in great spiritual turmoil, in 1654 and all his works, except *Apocrypha* (1652), were published in 1658 for the benefit of 'the Saints of Succeeding Ages'. Morgan Llwyd's final years were clouded by ill health, domestic tribulations and theological doubts, and he died, aged forty, in June 1659. He was buried in Rhos-ddu cemetery (the Welsh equivalent of

Bunhill Fields), where a monument was raised in his memory in 1912. By a tragic irony, a penitent letter, written by Vavasor Powell and designed to heal the rift between himself and his old colleague, arrived at Wrexham several weeks after Llwyd's death. [**DOCUMENT XII**] Walter Cradock, the elder statesman, died aged forty-nine in December 1659; Richard Symonds died in 1660 and Ambrose Mostyn in 1663. Of the leading Puritan activists only Henry Walter, who died in 1678, lived to see his sixtieth birthday, and of the principal Propagators only Vavasor Powell lived to witness (with bad grace) the joyful bell-ringing which greeted the return of the old order in 1660.

# 4.   'The Infection of the Times'

Godly reformation during these 'distempered and bedlam times' was by no means entirely dependent on state-subsidized propagation supported by warlords and saints. The turmoil of civil war, the lifting of censorship, the much wider availability of the Scriptures and the discovery of the virtues of toleration served to encourage the growth of religious plurality. According to Thomas Edwards, the arch-enemy of sectarians both real and imaginary, a myriad sects were busily 'spreading over this kingdom the gangrene of heresy and error'. As Puritanism fragmented into warring sects, new ideas, new concepts, and new heresies began to proliferate. Radical sects not only deplored the notion of maintaining preachers out of the public purse but also grappled with economic issues, the question of tithes and reform of the law. Beleaguered gentlemen and clergy were convinced that the new tub-preachers would prove a force for anarchy and they heaped ridicule on the 'gibberish' preached by the likes of Ananias the button-maker and Flash the cobbler. But although there were times when Wales seemed to be a Babel of discordant voices, the doctrines of the Levellers, Diggers, Ranters and Seekers, whose radical ideas threatened to 'turn the world upside down' in England, (51) had little or no influence on the Welsh, and the most serious threats to established order were the Baptists and the Quakers.

There were few avowed Baptists in Wales until evangelizing chaplains, radical soldiers and itinerant preachers began to propagate anti-paedobaptist doctrines (opposing infant baptism) during the civil wars. Baptists were especially strong in the army and Thomas Edwards claimed in 1646 that soldiers had been 'a preaching and dipping' in Breconshire and Radnorshire, and had 'vented many doctrines of Antinomianisme and Anabaptisme, and re-baptized hundreds in those Counties'. Even if we discount Edwards's proverbial gift for hyperbole, it is still evident that growing numbers of people on the Welsh borders, and certainly in Welsh-speaking parishes in Herefordshire, were turning their backs on the ungodly

world, forming communities of saints, and practising believers'
baptism. As royalist power crumbled along the Marches, groups of
Baptists went over to the offensive and made swift advances.

Baptists were divided into two distinct camps. The Particular, or
Calvinist, Baptists held fast to the doctrine of predestinarianism (the
belief that Christ's sacrifice on the Cross had been on behalf of the
elect), while General, or Arminian, Baptists believed that Christ had
died on the Cross for the whole of mankind. Both groups insisted that
only believers were eligible for Christian baptism, that total
immersion was the appropriate means of accepting believers into the
fold, and that personal experience of religion and liberty of conscience
were values to be highly cherished. The first successful expedition
was launched in 1646 by the General Baptists. Hugh Evans of Llan-
hir, Radnorshire, a man of deep religious convictions, persuaded
Jeremiah Ives, Arminian Baptist minister at Old Jewry, London, to
accompany him on a missionary enterprise in Radnorshire; he also
later engaged the services of Thomas Lamb, minister of Bell Alley
Church in London, in similar forays in Breconshire. The Act of
Propagation also proved a fillip to the Baptist cause. Mixed congregations of Baptists and Congregationalists worshipped together in
brotherly love in Montgomeryshire and Radnorshire and their commitment to the cause of saving souls was never less than wholehearted.

John Miles stood like a Colossus above all other Welsh Baptists in
this period. Miles was twenty-eight years old when he and Thomas
Proud were commissioned by the London Calvinistic Baptists in the
summer of 1649 to baptize believers in Glamorgan. An astute and
strong-willed man, Miles was a native of Newton-Clifford in
Herefordshire and had been educated at Brasenose College, Oxford.
During the years of civil strife he had served as either a soldier or a
chaplain with the parliamentary forces. How much Welsh he spoke
we cannot tell, but he was evidently the most Puritan of Puritans and
had a reputation of being rather stern and overbearing. He wisely
settled in the heavily puritanized Gower peninsula and began
baptizing adult believers in the parish of Ilston.

In many ways the history of early Welsh Baptists is the history of
John Miles and it was entirely fitting that a memorial to him, as the
founder of the Welsh Calvinist Baptist denomination, was erected
(and unveiled by David Lloyd George) in the parish of Ilston in June
1928. Miles, the evangelist and organizer, was nothing if not persistent, and although his desire to dominate others did not endear him
to everyone, those who were close to him and who benefited from his

advice and inspiration spoke of him with reverent awe. Baptist causes in south Wales were undeniably heavily dependent on his direction and commitment. His role as an Approver under the terms of the Propagation Act was clearly an advantage, for the finances and freedoms afforded by state-sponsored evangelization enabled several Baptist causes to prosper. By the summer of 1652 Miles had added four Calvinist closed communion churches — Hay-on-Wye, Llantrisant, Carmarthen and Abergavenny ('golden candlesticks', as he called them) — to the mother church at Ilston. The manner in which Miles and his disciples made sizeable inroads into Congregational territory, especially at Llanigon, Breconshire, angered rabid paedobaptists, but Miles remained unrepentant. Firmly in the saddle, he looked forward to further expansion.

From 1650 onwards 'Associations' or 'General Meetings' were held at irregular intervals in places like Ilston, Carmarthen, Abergavenny and Aberafan, and it was there that representatives offered advice or gave financial support to churches in difficulty, issued instructions pertaining to faith and conduct, and either disowned errant members or brought them to heel. Miles endeavoured to rule over his widely scattered flocks with grenadier-like efficiency, but this eventually proved impossible. Exercising effective surveillance over members who dwelt far from Ilston taxed his patience and resources, and he was obliged to relax some of his stricter injunctions and encourage less well-endowed preachers than possibly he would have liked to satisfy the spiritual needs of members in faraway branches. Miles's ministry, too, was riven by disputes concerning matters such as the nature of communion, the laying on of hands, the singing of psalms in services, and the validity of tithes.

At Ilston (for which reasonably full documentation exists), Miles and his colleagues established a strict routine of administration and worship in a bid to set up a united and fruitful fellowship. **[DOCUMENT XIII]** The pastor — Miles himself — was authorized to preach, reprove, administer ordinances, and excommunicate those who had succumbed to the wiles of Satan. The teacher (or prophet) was expected to instruct his flock in the Scriptures and eliminate heretical doctrines, while ordinary prophets were encouraged to exhort according to their lights. The advice of the ruling elder was sought on disciplinary matters and he was expected to keep the meeting place in good order. The deacon served communion, attended to financial matters, and ministered — assisted by well-disposed female members — to the poor. The regular round of worship in the parish church was not confined to sermons and prayers on the Sabbath; weekly meetings were held on Wednesdays, fast days on the first Wednesday of each month, and Sunday communion every third week. The small minority of members who brought the Baptist faith into disrepute by indulging in disorderly practices, cursing and swearing, drunkenness and sexual misdemeanours were summarily excommunicated.

Between 1649 and 1660, 261 Baptist members (153 women and 108 men) were enrolled at Ilston in response to Miles's drive for godly reformation. Apart from the parish of Ilston itself, most of them came from Bishopston, Llangennech, Llanelli, Swansea, Margam, Aberafan, Briton Ferry and Neath. The piety and radicalism of the Baptist faith were clearly attractive to middling orders, for there were squires, freeholders, stewards, portreeves and former soldiers among the recruits. If the 'Phillip Jones of Llangevellach' listed in the Ilston Churchbook was Col. Philip Jones, the most distinguished supporter of the Cromwellian establishment in south Wales, then Miles had a powerful friend to shield him and plead on his behalf. Names like 'Charity', 'Prudence' and 'Sage' within the Ilston fraternity indicate not only the debt owed by Baptists to their Puritan inheritance but also the lively presence of women. Popular participation in worship was encouraged by Baptists and this may account for the fact that women (59 per cent) far outnumbered men (41 per cent) in the gathered church at Ilston. Even though it is hard to believe that a martinet like Miles ignored gender divisions, women who had been denied a voice in the established church revelled in the opportunity to worship freely, debate, and participate in charitable work. Not least among the attractions of believers' baptism was that they could happily count themselves the equal of their husbands and other males in spiritual matters.

The very presence of Baptists rarely failed to excite comment and hostility and, as they began to make headway, clashes with their enemies were inevitable. The notion of adult baptism touched many raw nerves in a society in which the family was so highly prized. Affluent people knew full well that Baptist doctrines had profound implications for political authority, social status and property rights. Rightly or wrongly, the enemies of Baptists were convinced that anti-paedobaptists were determined to abolish the family unit, undermine the authority of ministers and magistrates, and erode the sanctity of private property. It was mischievously claimed that Baptists violated the sixth and seventh commandments by plunging near-naked candidates into icy rivers and ponds in mid-winter in the presence of a leering congregation. Inevitably, too, Baptists found themselves vulnerable to the slur of 'Munsterism' and 'Anabaptism', epithets which were synonymous with heresy, promiscuity, violence and anarchy. Strong-arm tactics employed by Capt. Jenkin Jones of Llanddeti in Breconshire caused much alarm in propertied circles and when he and his armed followers allegedly used force to abuse the rights and privileges of the burgesses of the corporation of Brecon, smear words such as 'Levellers' and 'John of Leyden' were invoked in order to link his deeds with the bizarre atrocities committed by fanatics in the Westphalian city of Münster in 1533–4. [DOCUMENT XIV] Joshua Thomas noted that Miles's vigorous proselytizing brought him under 'the scourge of the tongue', but he and his colleagues relished the opportunity to defend Baptist doctrines in public debates and literary skirmishes. David Davies, Baptist minister at Gelli-gaer, clashed violently in a public debate with no less an adversary than William Erbery, while a dispute in the parish church of Abergavenny in September 1653 between the redoubtable Baptist John Tombes of Leominster and John Cragge of Llantilio Pertholau persisted for nearly five hours. Such heated debates often led to acrimony, schism and fragmentation, but they were also a measure of the extent to which Baptists threatened to disrupt traditional society.

Baptists, in turn, were increasingly flayed by 'railing Rabshakehs who . . . never cease to blasphem the name, wayes, and precious Ministers of the Lord'. These were the Quakers, who had no qualms at all about giving arrogant Baptists a taste of their own medicine. John Miles believed that they were 'the Infection of the Times' and he was not alone in deploring the presence of such noisy, irreverent and troublesome newcomers. (19) Once Morgan Llwyd had sent emissaries to Swarthmoor Hall, near Ulverston, in July 1653, to gain a deeper understanding of the doctrines of the 'Children of the Light', the Quaker thrust westwards into Wales was bound to follow. Llwyd's interest in them is easily explained: there were obvious points of contact between the spiritual mysticism of Boehme and the Quaker doctrine of the inner light. He recognized them as kindred spirits in the sense that they, too, were seekers after the truth, but since they did not, in his view, embrace 'the whole truth', he never actually joined them, though he might well have done had he lived to witness the Restoration. Even in 1659 (the year of Llwyd's death), when fears of a Quaker-led militia aroused shuddering fear among the propertied classes, Llwyd was the only leading Puritan saint in Wales who pleaded for liberty of conscience for Quakers.

From 1653 onwards, Quakerism slowly but surely began to fill the vacuum left by the collapse of the millenarian cause along the Welsh borders. Many radicals who had spilt blood on battlefields in order to rid Wales of royal tyranny and prepare for the coming of 'King Jesus' and the rule of the saints saw in Quakerism fresh hopes of stiffening the Good Old Cause. Growing numbers of dissatisfied people, burdened perhaps by guilt, torment, resentment and disillusionment, had passed from church to conventicle, and from radical sect to radical sect, only to find each one wanting. Such seekers found peace of mind in the bosom of Quakerism. This process can be briefly illustrated by reference to the spiritual odyssey of two men whose sense of insecurity and despair swept them into the movement. Born in July 1627, Thomas Wynne was a freeholder's son from the upland parish of Ysgeifiog in Flintshire. [**DOCUMENT XV**] He was an uncommonly restless young man who, ridden with guilt and confusion, despaired of ever being able to overcome his doubts, sins and temptations. In his quest for truth during the civil wars, he consulted well-regarded Puritan ministers and 'professors', none of whom, alas, could provide adequate answers to his queries. Sometime in the mid-1650s, however, Wynne's stressful pilgrimage came to an end when the Quaker message convinced him that he who obeyed the light of Christ within might attain perfection. When he discovered the extraordinary power of the inner light, his limbs trembled and his body shook uncontrollably. His ecstatic account of his spiritual transformation ranks among the most memorable expressions of personal revelation in Stuart Wales. The light of truth also stirred the imagination of Richard Davies, a feltmaker from Cloddiau Cochion, near Welshpool, and his vivid autobiography — eight editions of which were published by 1840 — provides an invaluable mirror of the soul of a man who served the Quaker cause for over fifty years. (6) In his teens he was inspired by the teachings of Vavasor Powell, who urged him to attend Congregational meetings and read the Scriptures. But Davies found no true comfort in the words of his mentor and used to retire to secluded woods to examine his soul and pray. Powell was mortified when, in 1657, his young protégé defected to the Quakers, but Davies could only wonder at the 'marvellous Light' which had brought him enormous joy and peace of mind.

Churchmen and Puritans alike were convinced that Quakers constituted the most dangerous threat to the well-being of the Protestant faith and the social and political fabric. The principal doctrine of the Quakers — to which all else was deemed subordinate — was the notion of the inner light. Based on scriptural evidence in John 1:9, this doctrine told of the light which had come into the world in the person of Jesus of Nazareth. The unerring power of the anointing within was capable of transforming vulnerable and distressed pilgrims into brave and determined zealots who could never be intimidated into silence, obedience or flight. All Quakers abhorred formalism, idolatry and superstition. Their contempt for the established 'visible' churches ('steeplehouses' as they called them) was plain to see. They knew their Bibles well — and hugely respected the Word of God — but they denied the infallibility of the Scriptures. They were violently anti-establishment: ministers were corrupt hirelings, tithes were a Jewish burden, oaths were contrary to Scripture; universities were bastions of privilege. Violating accepted codes of honour was second nature to them. Social etiquette and convention were abandoned as they used the pronouns of address *ti* (thee) and *tithe* (thou), and refused to remove their hats or bow or curtsy in the presence of their superiors. When Richard Davies appeared behatted before the High Sheriff and magistrates of Montgomeryshire, they were nonplussed by his temerity and 'stood as People in amaze'. The chagrin which hat-wearing provoked in gentry circles has recently been likened to the impact once felt in America when a black man called a white woman by her first name. Quakers deplored the pride, selfishness and carnal pleasures which characterized the lives of affluent gentlemen, and there was a strong element of spiritual and social egalitarianism in their doctrines and deeds.

From around 1654 onwards, John ap John, the Ruabon yeoman who never swerved from the Quaker witness for over forty years, began organizing ministerial missions. He and his colleagues sensibly devoted their energies to winning converts in areas where the soil had been liberally watered by Puritan evangelists. Inadvertently, Puritan preachers like Cradock, Erbery and Mostyn had prepared the way for them by deriding outward forms of worship like the Prayer Book, holy days, church festivals and symbols of all kinds. Quaker preachers normally travelled in pairs, and as they moved southwards they tempted restless and vulnerable people, seduced seekers, and collided with enemies. Thomas Holme, the Kendal weaver, rejoiced loudly whenever Baptist congregations in rural mid Wales were raided and 'broken into pieces'. The notion of universal redemption was clearly attractive, and Quakers cleverly poured scorn on the rigid Calvinism of their Puritan predecessors. They also used metaphors calculated to appeal to rural folk: hearers were urged to plough, plant, harvest and thresh in the name of Christ. Given a free hand by their leaders, they made for towns, fairs, markets and churches, where people assembled in considerable numbers and where they were assured of a hearing.

Wherever Quakers assembled there was invariably public disorder. Their public worship was deliberately calculated to shock: eerie silences were punctuated by raucous expressions of personal revelation and disturbing bouts of quaking, roaring and trembling. Puritan ministers were thrown off balance when hectoring Quakers entered their churches and humiliated them by calling them dumb dogs, hirelings and false prophets. Joshua Miller of Cardiff was appalled by the crude 'Billingsgate' language employed by his adversary, Francis Gawler, a prickly and combative Quaker who used to inform Puritan preachers that the mark of the Beast was clearly imprinted on their foreheads. Quakers thrived on public disputes and confrontations. During George Fox's tour of Wales in 1657, he and John ap John would march up and down main streets, encouraging onlookers to hearken to the inward voice and inviting abuse and harassment by preaching in an aggressive fashion. It was not unusual for travelling Quakers to seek attention — not to say public ridicule — by 'going naked for a sign' or appearing in sackcloth. [**DOCUMENT XVI**] In spite of the envy, abuse and hatred which Quakers evoked, they brought colour and vitality to spiritual life in Wales. All the indications are that to be a Quaker in this period was a truly liberating — even exhilarating — experience.

Quaker missionaries made repeated sorties into south Wales and achieved ominous gains. John and Mabel Camm informed Margaret Fell in March 1655 of 'great meettinges in South Wales . . . some magistrates and justices hath meettinges at their houses and this is an incorragement to others.' No preachers were more persistent and tenacious than the Quakers and although the number of their converts was still small, they were considered a serious menace by landlords, ministers and public officials. A major turning-point occurred in the summer of 1657 when the charismatic figure of George Fox arrived. His aim was to infuse the Quaker expansion in Wales with new energy and also to repair the damage caused to the reputation of the movement by James Nayler's celebrated débâcle at Bristol the previous autumn. Although Fox's inability to preach in Welsh was a grave obstacle (as indeed in the case of John Wesley in the eighteenth century), he nevertheless beguiled hearers with his hypnotic eyes and powerful voice, displayed his proverbial gift for prophecy, and confounded many enemies during his two-month tour of the thirteen counties of Wales. It was by no means a triumphal progress — 'wicked thievish people' and truculent magistrates were particularly hostile in north Wales — but he and his companion, John ap John, were well received in bilingual towns like Cardiff, Haverfordwest, Tenby and Pontypool, where Quakers had already established themselves. Since most of the material in Fox's captivating journal was dictated with the benefit of hindsight, it may well be that it offers a misleading perspective in that the account of the journey does less than justice to John ap John. One suspects that the tour was the making of John ap John; it was he who shouldered the main burden of preaching, incurred the wrath of ministers and magistrates, and bore the foul abuse of his compatriots. (21) Nevertheless, Fox's very presence enabled the movement to gather pace and strength. It drew support largely from smaller squires and yeomen in rural communities and small traders, craftsmen and artisans in the towns.

Women figured prominently in the Quaker mission in Wales and were encouraged to evangelize as freely as men. They showed remarkable energy and belligerency in the face of fierce opposition. Elizabeth Holme evangelized with such persistence in Cardiff and Swansea that the gaoler of the notorious 'dark house' at Swansea was obliged to chain her by the leg as far as possible from the prison window in order to prevent her from berating Puritan ministers as they passed by. Dorcas Erbery, William's daughter, was a devotee of James Nayler and was viciously punished for her part in her hero's attempt to re-enact Christ's entry into Jerusalem; undeterred, she returned to Cardiff to mobilize support and heap ridicule on salaried ministers. The sheer persistence and fearless courage of Alice Birkett brought out the worst in people: she was stripped naked, stoned and publicly humiliated in Llandaff churchyard. Such women paid the price for a fuller share in the propagation of the gospel and church life: for periods of time they were locked in squalid prisons barely fit for beasts let alone prisoners of conscience.

Unlike their modern descendants, the Quakers of the 1650s were by no means gentle, meek and patient men and women. On the contrary, they were radical, turbulent and bellicose people who proclaimed their message with fearless candour. As befitted saints who had taken up arms against the Antichrist, they riddled their sermons and tracts with military metaphors. There were far more hawks than doves in their ranks. Arise Evans, the ardent royalist prophet, claimed in 1660 that Quakers had never been reluctant to shed blood in the name of parliamentary liberty. In rural Merioneth, the redoubtable Robert Owen of Dolserau had no qualms about using the arm of flesh as a soldier, sequestrator and commissioner of taxes. Former soldiers were popular agitators in Cardiff: Francis Gawler had served as an officer in the New Model Army and Matthew Gibbon of Moulton, in the parish of Llancarfan, lost an arm in the service of the parliamentary cause. Such men were believed to be bent on whittling away the powers of magistrates and ministers, and pursuing sectional interests which would undoubtedly contribute to further division and strife.

Quakers, therefore, aroused more hostility and fear than any other radical sect in this period. Their inflammatory language, outrageous codes of behaviour and bellicose postures made them much more than simply squalid nuisances. Churchmen and Puritans closed ranks against them because they feared that such dangerous malcontents would never rest until the world was well and truly turned upside down. Desperate efforts were made to publicize adverse images of the Quakers: as sorcerers, witches, Levellers, heretics and crypto-Papists. Even sweet-tempered Puritan ministers were so mortified by baiting Quakers that they resorted to violence. Stephen Hughes boxed the ears of a hectoring Quaker, while Walter Cradock found his patience taxed beyond endurance by the impudent taunts of Francis Gawler. 'Get thee behind me Satan', he cried as he whipped Gawler's horse, 'I have hearkened to thee, but now do deny thee, thou dost torment me day and night. I speak not to thee Gawler, but to the devil in thee.' Richard Davies freely admitted that Quakers were always cast in an unfavourable light because they were considered 'a dangerous sort of people'. Such a tainted faith could not be allowed to prosper and local magistrates who implemented harsh and repressive measures against Quakers were universally applauded.

# 5.   'This Cloud of Affliction'

By 1659 it was not simply fear of the consequences of Quakerism which prompted the majority of Welsh people to yearn for the restoration of the exiled Stuart monarch. For nearly two decades Wales had been 'tossed in a blanket'. Two bitter and bloody civil wars had been fought, a king of reputedly 'Brythonic' descent had been publicly topped, estates had been confiscated, stately homes pillaged and burnt, and crippling taxes and fines imposed. All this had proved a nightmarish experience for royalists and churchmen. Where once there were long-established patrician families, there were now upwardly mobile commoners who, with the aid of writs, pikes, bayonets and pistols, heaped indignities upon their masters. Where formerly there were university-trained and ordained clergymen, there were now blacksmiths, millers and tailors masquerading as preachers in the pulpit. Although a small number of gentry families — for pragmatic or cynical reasons — had been happy to make common cause with the republican administration and even enjoy cordial relations with Puritan governors, the hastily conceived and oppressive constitutional experiments embarked on by Cromwell (notably the ill-starred Major-Generals' scheme in 1655–6), coupled with what poets called 'the power of the committee', not only failed to win the support of the traditional ruling classes but also prompted many of them to thirst for revenge. There was much anger and resentment, too, in the hearts of clergymen, especially those who had suffered the indignity of ejection from their livings. The church which they cherished had been torn asunder by loathsome schismatics who had robbed priests of their authority and pride, expelled the old liturgy, and prohibited much-loved customs and recreations. 'For precious balme', mourned Rowland Watkyns, rector of Llanfrynach, 'we have but kitchen-stuffe.' Even more galling was the knowledge that there were charlatans, trimmers, hypocrites and self-seekers in Puritan ranks, and tales of illegal trafficking in ecclesiastical revenues made churchmen all the more determined to bring the 'ill times' to a swift end.

The Puritan manifesto had proved repugnant to the common man. Evangelists were met either with sullen indifference or stubborn hostility. Major-General Charles Fleetwood wearily confessed that the Welsh had 'envenomed hearts' against Puritan values, and this was particularly true of the inhabitants of more sheltered counties in the north and west. Col. John Jones of Maesygarnedd was not simply teasing Morgan Llwyd when he said of his native county, 'where is there more sine to encounter wth, where more ignorance, where more hatred to the people of god? Where word saint more scorned? than in Merionethshire.' Even in Monmouthshire, where William Wroth's faithful disciples had laboured mightily on behalf of the Puritan cause, Roundheads were vilified by local rhymesters for reducing Wales to 'a living hell'. Nowhere is the general antipathy towards Puritanism more graphically portrayed than in the poetry of the times: epithets such as 'bastards', 'king-killers', 'cuckolds', 'the scum of the world', 'ugly seducers' and 'shiny-arsed weavers' gave expression to the deep sense of bitterness and hatred which informed popular opinion. Even as the so-called Puritan Revolution degenerated into mutual recrimination and sordid factionalism, ardent royalists and churchmen looked forward to the opportunity to pay off old scores.

News of the arrival of the Merry Monarch at Dover in May 1660 was greeted with delirious joy in Wales. The demise of republican rule, wrote Sarah Wynne of Gwydir, was 'such a mercy that we canot a nufe prise it'. King Charles II, it was widely proclaimed, was a heaven-sent saviour who promised a return to the 'good old days'. Wales echoed to the incessant pealing of bells and the firing of cannon as people celebrated the downfall of a regime which had exercised a harsh and unwelcome domination over their lives. Puritans, for their part, were bewildered and sad. It was hard for them to understand why the Revolution had collapsed so ignominiously. Had Providence spat in their faces? Was the glorious reformation doomed to failure? Was the return of the monarch a divine punishment? These were some of the unresolved questions which troubled their consciences as the dark days of persecution beckoned.

Although Welsh separatists and radicals were a loosely knit and poorly organized group by 1660, jittery magistrates kept well-known malcontents under close surveillance. The 'Good Old Cause' was far from dead, particularly in the towns of south Wales where old republican sympathies remained strong and where radical sectarians and soldiers were not disposed to abandon hard-earned freedoms and privileges. Plots and risings were expected, and fears that former soldiers were dusting off their uniforms and preparing for renewed combat were not entirely fanciful. Supporters of the restored regime were convinced that the potential for insurrection was present in Wales and that Puritan conventicles were nurseries of sedition and strife. Deputy lieutenants throughout Wales were ordered to round up 'disaffected' people, impound caches of arms and barrels of powder, and administer the oaths of supremacy and allegiance to all suspects. Letters to and from former rebels were intercepted and opened. There was undoubtedly widespread fear of conspiracy, assassination and rebellion.

The extreme radicalism of the Quakers meant that they were marked men. According to Joseph Besse, violence against Quakers was so acute in 1660 that 'the very Name of a Quaker exposed a Man to the Loss of his Liberty'. A violent persecutor of Quakers at Carmarthen claimed that he was at liberty to do his worst 'now the king being come'. Moth-eaten recusancy and vagrancy statutes dating back to Elizabethan times were discovered by the authorities and used against Quaker preachers. Soon tiny and pestilential gaols in towns like Cardiff, Presteigne, Swansea and Welshpool were filled to overflowing with Quakers whose refusal to desist from preaching or to take the oath of allegiance was construed as a mark of disloyalty. Adults and children mocked them by crying repeatedly 'Quaker! Quaker! Quaker!', particularly when their homes were raided, ransacked and looted by constables armed with swords, staves and pistols. In fact, all political suspects were subjected to nocturnal raids by officers searching for arms. Sir Matthew Price, High Sheriff of Montgomeryshire, claimed that 'fanatics' in his county 'gave one another bread on a rapier's point' and possessed 'concealed arms and long knives'. Not surprisingly, Vavasor Powell, the arch-demon of the Puritan cause in mid Wales, was swiftly rounded up and placed under lock and key in July 1660. Save for a brief period of ten months, Powell was to spend the rest of his days in captivity. He died, aged fifty-three, in Caronne House (awaiting the completion of the new Fleet prison) in October 1670 and lies in an unknown grave in Bunhill Fields, London. It was entirely characteristic of this indomitable man that he should have penned a work memorably entitled *Bird in the Cage, Chirping* (1661) whilst languishing in the Fleet: 'let us redeem time', he urged his followers, 'be watchful and sober, keeping our lights burning, our Lamps shining, our Loyns girded, our Consciences awakned, and our garments unstained, and our Spiritual armour constantly on, and closely girt.'

Elsewhere in Wales, militant Roundheads were placed on the defensive or robbed of their liberty. In Llŷn, Richard Edwards of Nanhoron — considered 'a man of close and shrewd parts and of dangerous principles' — and John Williams of Ty'n-y-coed were kept under strict surveillance, not least because they were known to have corresponded with Vavasor Powell and other insurgents in London. Nor had Capt. Jenkin Jones of Llanddeti abandoned his republican convictions. When a posse of soldiers was ordered to disperse one of his Baptist congregations, Jones urged his disciples to defy them. Blood was shed in the ensuing skirmish and Jones declared loudly that the King's reign would prove short-lived since the saints would 'have another turne' before Michaelmas. But as Jones was marched off to Carmarthen gaol, stone-throwing mobs publicly demonstrated the strength of pro-monarchist feeling. He was released shortly afterwards, but since he refused to draw in his horns he was imprisoned a second time. No one knows what became of Jones, but there is not a shadow of doubt that he was not the kind of man to betray his republican allies. Nor did the Welsh regicide, Col. John Jones of Maesygarnedd, express any regrets for having signed the death warrant of Charles I. He likened the sled which dragged him from Newgate prison to the gallows at Charing Cross on 17 October to Elijah's fiery chariot, and his final prayer conveyed the sentiments of a man utterly certain of his own redemption and of the validity of the 'Good Old Cause'. [DOCUMENT XVII]

Once the most extreme and libertarian radical separatists had been incarcerated, attention turned to the vexed question of establishing a religious polity based on the alliance of church and state. Following his return from exile Charles II made conciliatory noises which, whether sincere or not, seemed to augur well for the future of Dissent. He was anxious to arrive at a compromise church settlement which would please moderate episcopalians and moderate Presbyterians. Congregationalists, of course, had no wish to be incorporated within a national church and no one in authority was disposed to reach an understanding with contumacious Baptists and Quakers. Liberal sentiments voiced by the King in the Declaration of Breda were endorsed by the Convention Parliament and the Savoy Conference of April–July 1661 briefly raised the hopes of the Presbyterians. But the Cavalier Parliament which assembled in May 1661 was dominated by unforgiving royalists who were so hostile to Puritans, sectaries and republicans that all proposals involving comprehension were bound to be crushed. Eaten up with hatred and thoughts of vengeance,

Cavaliers were not prepared to forget past injustices and injuries. The tide of Anglican resentment was running particularly strongly in north Wales, where the nobility and gentry, purporting to represent the interests of the inhabitants of six counties, called on the King to reintroduce 'all those good and wholesome Laws for uniformity in Religion'. Indignities suffered at the hands of Philip Jones and his ruling clique also prompted angry royalists and vindictive churchmen in south Wales to demand that the harshest possible religious and civil disabilities be imposed upon old adversaries.

On 19 May 1662 the Act of Uniformity received the royal assent. It was designed to exclude non-Anglicans from all positions in the church, schools and universities. All clergymen were required by the Sabbath prior to 24 August (St Bartholomew's Day) to make a public declaration of their 'unfeigned assent and consent' to the contents of the newly revised Book of Common Prayer. Those who refused were to be deprived of their livings. By declaring that hence-forth there were to be two religions, the Act of Uniformity destroyed the old Puritan dream of reforming the established church from within. It created an 'us' and 'them' mentality which marked the final parting of the ways between conformists and non-conformists. Yet it must be emphasized that 'Black Bartholomew Day', traditionally associated with the expulsion of Puritan ministers, does not carry the same resonance in Wales as it does in England. There was no mass exodus in Wales on that date simply because the majority of recalci-trant ministers had already voted with their feet long before the deadline. Although it marked the official genesis of modern Welsh Dissent, the year 1662 in practice was the final scene in a drama which had reached its climax as early as the summer of 1660. Of 130 Puritan ministers who lost their livings, 95 (73 per cent) had been expelled before the Act of Uniformity was passed. Having read the portents, many of them had quietly vacated their livings, to be replaced either by clergymen who had been previously ejected by lay commissioners under the terms of the Propagation Act or by fresh nominees. There were, therefore, precious few heroes or martyrs in Wales in August 1662.

The highest number of ejections — Glamorgan (23), Breconshire (14), Montgomeryshire (13), Denbighshire (11), Pembrokeshire (11) and Monmouthshire (10) — occurred in those counties where Pur-itanism had prospered best and where the major work of the pro-pagators had been accomplished. It was perhaps natural for the victims of persecution in the 1650s to give their enemies a taste of their own medicine once the old order had been restored. But efforts were also made to wean those who were not unduly troubled by Puritan scruples from the vanquished radical cause. Many ministers were content to come to terms with the new regime so long as this enabled them to retain their livings. Some trimmers scrambled to ingratiate themselves with royalists and it was ultimately to some advantage for Dissent that Pliable and Worldly-Wiseman were not prepared to make heavy sacrifices by holding fast to the separatist movement. Nor should we forget that Puritanism did not always run strongly in families. Manasseh and Mordecai Matthews, sons of the Puritan minister Marmaduke, both conformed to the established church and were rewarded with livings. Many others, especially Presbyterians, accepted the logic of swimming with the tide.

Fear of persecution was insufficient to persuade fervent Puritans to forsake old allegiances. Most of them responded to the challenge with considerable spirit and courage. Before he vanished from Dissenting records, Jenkin Jones fired a bullet through the door of his local parish church (the bullet can be seen in the Brecknock Museum) and bitterly cursed the 'old whore of Babylon' which had regained its primacy. Congregationalists and Baptists made no secret of their contempt for the Prayer Book and those who neglected to use it were often forced to run the gauntlet of irate parishioners. [DOCUMENT XVIII] Thomas Warren of Narberth publicly informed his parishioners that the Prayer Book was 'a packett of lies and the Invention of Man', while Christopher Jackson, rector of Llanddewi Felffre, mixed pages from the Prayer Book with tobacco in his pipe and warned all and sundry that only the wicked welcomed the return of the King. Such men of 'scrupulous conscience' were determined to remain a prickly thorn in the flesh of the Church of England. Characteristically, Vavasor Powell believed that harassment and persecution could prove the salvation of Dissent: 'the heat of prosperity would have burnt us, if God had not sent this Cloud of affliction to cover us.' He knew better than most that the ultimate victory of Dissent was assured.

The Cavalier Parliament, which first met in May 1661 and lasted for eighteen years, passed a series of severe and reactionary penal statutes collectively called the Clarendon Code. These enactments drastically curtailed the religious and civil rights of Dissenters and even threatened them with financial ruin, imprisonment and death. Their aim, in short, was to wipe out Dissent. The first measure, the Corporation Act of December 1661, declared that all municipal officials were expected to swear oaths of allegiance and non-resistance to the Crown and to partake of the Anglican sacrament. In other words, it was made abundantly clear that only church communicants were politically acceptable; in the eyes of the law, non-conformists were not 'one of us'. Security measures were then tightened against turbulent Quakers: in May 1662 a specially designed Quaker Act prohibited meetings of five or more Quakers and imposed stiff penalties on those who refused to swear oaths. But the authorities continued to smell conspiracy and rebellion on the wind and this left them with no choice but to extend the provisions of the Quaker Act in order to make life intolerable for all Dissenters. In May 1664 the First Conventicle Act prohibited more than five persons above the age of sixteen from attending any meetings not conducted in accordance with the liturgy of the Church of England. Offenders were liable to a fine of £5 or three months in prison. A second offence meant that the penalty was doubled. A third offence was punishable by a fine of £100 or transportation for seven years.

The next step was to make life hazardous for Dissenting ministers whose severance from the church, so churchmen argued, was provoked by pride, prejudice, malice and sedition. The Five Mile Act, passed in October 1665, was designed to destroy their influence in towns. It prohibited Dissenting ministers who had refused to swear the necessary oaths and declarations from teaching and preaching within five miles of any city or borough or corporate town or wherever they had formerly exercised their ministry. The First Conventicle Act of 1664 had been a short-term expedient which expired on 1 March 1669. However, returns included in a survey of religion commissioned by Archbishop Sheldon in June of the latter year convinced Parliament that a much tougher assault on conventicles was required. In May 1670 a much more severe measure, designed to bring financial ruin to Dissent, entered the statute books. The Second Conventicle Act — called 'the quintessence of arbitrary malice' by Marvell — imposed a system of fines upon Dissenting worshippers, beginning with five shillings, a penalty which doubled with each offence. Householders and officiating ministers who invited conventiclers to their homes were liable to a fine of £20 for a first offence and £40 for each subsequent transgression. Previous loopholes (gleefully exploited by the craftiest Dissenters) were closed by enabling a single magistrate, rather than two, to convict on the basis of a confession or the oaths of two witnesses or circumstantial evidence. The act also encouraged informers to betray friends by furnishing magistrates with information which might lead to a successful prosecution; a third of the fine levied on the offender was paid to the informer. Lazy magistrates also received a sharp dig in the ribs; those who neglected to prosecute conventiclers were made liable to a fine of £100.

In 1673 Charles II was compelled by Parliament to accept the Test Act, a measure chiefly designed to curb dangerous Roman Catholics. But it also drove Dissenters out of public life by requiring those who aspired to office under the Crown to receive the Anglican sacrament and swear loyalty to the King. The drive to re-establish one church and to eliminate Dissent had thus begun in earnest. Welsh Dissenters were confronted by a dispiriting array of penal laws whose avowed aim was abundantly clear: to inflict upon them untold pain, suffering and humiliation. Dissent was equated with fanaticism and rebellion, for memories of the Puritan sword died hard. Even the most devout and stubborn Dissenters must have been profoundly alarmed by such repressive measures; all of them were now required to be watchful, patient and resolute.

Although it would be grossly unjust to make light of the privations suffered by Dissenters during the period 1660–89, it must be borne in mind that the statutes which were intended to disrupt the organization of Dissenting conventicles and destroy all their hopes of building a secure future needed to be enforced effectively by prelates, clergymen, magistrates and their servants. The truth is that persecution was fitful rather than endemic. It varied from diocese to diocese, from parish to parish, and from year to year. External pressure was invariably a vital consideration. Alarmist reports of plots and risings or bubbling anti-Popish passions often led to renewed and violent activity against clandestine assemblies. The evidence strongly suggests that repressive measures were most rigorously enforced in 1660–7, 1670–1 and 1681–6. These were years when fears of conspiracy, assassination, rebellion and war prompted bishops, priests and justices to track down conventicles and bring illegal worshippers before the courts. At other times, harassment was intermittent and usually subject to external stimuli. When rigorously implemented, the Clarendon Code occasioned much pain and discomfort, but the afflictions endured by Welsh Dissenters do not brook comparison with the grievous atrocities visited upon the Huguenots in France.

Local initiatives were crucial in the campaign to dragoon Dissenters into conformity. Much depended on the predilections, will-power and energy of bishops. It boded ill for Dissent that Welsh bishops in the Restoration period were hand-picked royalists and Laudians who mourned the death of 'blessed Charles', viewed the established church as the sole legitimate dispenser of the means of salvation, and loathed schism, division and heresy. Dissent was never strong in the diocese of Bangor in this period, partly because bishops were so tenacious in defending the rights of the Church. Bishop William Roberts (1660–5), who had suffered rough treatment at the hands of men of inferior birth during the revolutionary period, so despised the name of 'the usurper Cromwell' that he did his utmost to strengthen the Anglican cause. His successor Robert Morgan (1665–73) loathed the 'phantastick revelations' peddled by self-styled saints, while Humphrey Lloyd (1673–89) was so hostile to Dissenters that he refused to support the laudable efforts of Thomas Gouge and Stephen Hughes to raise funds to publish a new edition of the Welsh Bible. At St Asaph, Bishop George Griffith (1660–6), who had boldly crossed swords with Vavasor Powell during the Interregnum, stoutly defended the need for a common liturgy and the fulfilment of catechetical duties. On his arrival at St Asaph in 1680, Bishop William Lloyd made conciliatory gestures to Dissenters and used his best endeavours to win their affections by conducting lengthy, if inconclusive, public debates in market towns like Llanfyllin, Oswestry and Welshpool. But when he discovered that gentle means were insufficient to bend them to his will, he pursued a much more vigorous and repressive policy against those 'bloody wretches' whose minds and hearts had been 'horribly poisoned by one Vavasor Powell'. In the penurious diocese of Llandaff, Lloyd's namesake (1675–9), the last Welshman to govern the diocese for two centuries, ruled with an iron hand, as sectaries found to their cost. However, no prelate nursed more violent prejudices against Dissent than William Lucy, a native of Hampshire who, at the age of sixty-eight, was appointed Bishop of St David's in 1660. Convinced that Dissent and treason were synonymous, he was a firm believer in the spirit of the Clarendon Code. He stood on no ceremony in his treatment of truculent sectaries and his epitaph is an eloquent (and concrete) tribute to his labours: 'Schismatis et Haeresium averruncator strenuus' (Vigorous banisher of schism and heresies).

Even such zealous and uncompromising men soon discovered that bringing Dissenters to heel was no easy task. Since the Conventicle Acts did not punish those who absented themselves from church, it was left to the consistory courts to prosecute habitual absentees, especially those who failed to celebrate Easter communion and neglected to send their children to be catechized. But the teeth of the Church courts were lamentably blunt. As Church Act Books demonstrate, their powers had ceased to matter. Penances were imposed and mulish absentees were excommunicated in large numbers, but penalties which denied offenders the right to communion in church were easily borne by those who had already forsaken Anglicanism. Names of regular offenders were listed so frequently by clerks that the sanction evidently lacked clout. Infuriated by the impotence of the church courts, Bishop Lucy had good cause to deplore 'those evill principles formerly instilld during ye late rebellion'. [DOCUMENT XIX] Churchwardens at Llandysilio in Carmarthenshire complained bitterly in 1684 that Dissenters who had been presented on several occasions 'yett escape unpunished', whilst churchwardens at Llandysul in Cardiganshire wearily observed that local Baptists sniggered at the sentence of excommunication and 'do not value it at [all]'. Even so, there were means available by which the mandate of church courts could be reinforced by the secular authorities. If a bishop so wished, he could send a *significavit* to the Court of Chancery in order to obtain a writ of excommunication against a stubborn Dissenter. This empowered a sheriff to imprison the offender until he repented, agreed to obey the diktats of the court and paid the costs of the suit. Such writs, however, entailed byzantine legal complications and were forbiddingly expensive, so much so that they were normally used only against rebellious Baptists and Quakers.

The rigorous implementation of the penal code was also determined by the extent to which magistrates were prepared to carry out the law. Those who were a constant prey to fears of further revolutionary turmoil were not averse to authorizing severe harassment. Some of them were vengeful and brutal, especially when stubborn or impudent Quakers courted trouble. Memories of the oppressive rule of 'Arbitrary and Republican Hoghens Moghens' were so fresh that aggrieved gentry could not ignore the presence of potential rebels. Those who bore personal grudges against former Puritans revelled in the coercive power of the state: 'we have the sword of power in our hands', rejoiced a violent magistrate from Oswestry, 'and by the grace of God, I will root you out of the country.' Small wonder that a Brawdy (Pembs.) husbandman, appalled by the manner in which magistrates treated Peregrine Phillips, the Congregationalist minister, declared in 1684 that 'he cared not a turd for any Justice of the peace'. The worst malice was reserved for Quakers. [DOCUMENT XX] When William Morton, a former royalist soldier and Chief Justice of the Carmarthen Circuit of the Court of the Great Sessions, ordered hats to be removed from the heads of Quaker prisoners, only to find that the offenders proceeded to cover their heads with their uppermost garments, he abused them foully and behaved 'like a Madd man bereaved of all naturall senses'. At Bala Assizes in August 1676 seven stubborn Quakers were confronted by the granite-faced Justice Thomas Walcott, who duly informed them that, unless they repented, the ancient writ 'for the burning of heretics' would be brought against them at the next assizes, thereby enabling the authorities to hang and quarter the men and burn to death the women. When small groups of Quakers at Cil-y-cwm and Llandingad in Carmarthenshire objected to the exorbitant poll tax imposed in 1690 by the local magistrate and commissioner of the poll tax, Roger Manwaring of Llandovery (great-grandson of the celebrated Vicar Prichard), he tore up their petition and cried 'Hang them!'

The very fact that many magistrates were remiss and lazy helped to soften the rigours of the law. Unless they were prodded into action by their superiors, they seldom bestirred themselves. Treatment of offenders tended to vary widely from county to county, much to the fury of diligent bishops and vengeful gentry. In March 1675 Robert Wynne, a magistrate of Gwnnodl, Glyndyfrdwy, was so disconcerted by the behaviour of forty Merioneth Quakers standing silently 'like beasts in a markett' and gazing upon one another 'like fooles in Bedlam' that he sought to stir local justices into more vigorous action against conventiclers. There were also humane magistrates who heartily detested the penal code and refused to proceed against well-regarded or peaceful Dissenters. Influential magistrates were able to plead on behalf of offenders and either impose lenient sentences or turn a blind eye to their activities. Even the notorious George Jeffreys of Acton, who referred disparagingly to those with 'the twang of fanaticism in their noses', dealt leniently with the likes of the Presbyterian Philip Henry. In west Glamorgan several leading gentry families like the Mansells of Margam and Briton Ferry and the Hobys of Neath were so well disposed towards local Dissenters that devotees of the church in the Vale of Glamorgan bitterly claimed that conventicles 'abound in the western parts, and . . . we could not well remedy the same without giving some disgust to the deputy lieutenants and justices of the peace of those limits'. In Flintshire Sir John Trevor of Trefalun offered refuge to William Jones, who had been forced to leave Denbigh for violating the Five Mile Act, while in Pembrokeshire the Owens of Orielton and the Perrots of Haroldston were warmly disposed towards Peregrine Phillips, ejected minister of Llangwm and Freystrop. Even among the Quakers there were occasions when affluent and influential gentlemen like Charles and Thomas Lloyd of Dolobran, Montgomeryshire, were able to shield their followers from the worst rigours of the law.

The extent to which the penal code was severely enforced was also often determined by the opinion of local citizens whose views could work in favour of Dissenters. Well-regarded and decent neighbours, particularly if they were moderate Presbyterians or Congregational-ists, were allowed to live almost as normally as members of the church and it would be wrong to assume that they were hag-ridden with anxiety and fearful of violence against them throughout this period. Neighbours and friends of Dissenters often refused to assist officers because they could see no evil in them, and churchwardens and constables were deliberately remiss for humanitarian reasons. Some even protected them by warning them of the identity and where-abouts of informers. The aims of the Second Conventicle Act were often nullified by the deep sense of shame and outrage felt by local inhabitants as a result of the behaviour of prying informers who had no scruples about perjuring themselves in court. Informers were widely detested: Edmond Harris, a particularly obnoxious spy in Dissenting circles in Pembrokeshire, was dubbed 'the Grand Informer' by local Quakers, and the activities of Robert Sowtrell, a Shrewsbury cooper who terrorized Quakers in mid Wales by loudly declaring that 'if he should live to the Age of Methuselah he would continue to be the Quakers' Tormentor', often proved counter-productive. Richard Davies tells us of a hapless Welshpool weaver who was snubbed by magistrates and boycotted by his neighbours because of his mischief-making and greed. **[DOCUMENT XXI]** When goods seized from the Quaker Thomas Simmonds of Puncheston in Pembrokeshire were distributed by local officials among the poor, they refused to accept them because Simmonds had always been so generous to all his neighbours.

The nature and extent of persecution were also determined by the willingness of Dissenters (except Quakers, who always bore public witness to their faith) to resort to a variety of evasive or diversionary tactics. This was not cowardice on their part; such stratagems simply betokened a fierce determination to survive and prosper. Some of them relished playing cat-and-mouse with dyspeptic sheriffs and blundering constables, nimbly outwitting them by keeping on the move, varying the location of conventicles, rearranging the time of meetings at the eleventh hour, and covering their tracks extremely well. Henry Maurice claimed that beleaguered Dissenters in the Llŷn peninsula were so fearful that 'they came together very late in the night'. Even heavy snow could not deter fervent Baptists from assembling at night in secluded woods near Maesyberllan in Breconshire. Vigilant sentries were posted and elaborate escape-routes devised. When a substantial congregation of around a hundred worshippers at Wrexham was surprised by a detachment of militia in February 1665, the overwhelming majority of them escaped through a back entrance. Secret and secluded locations were often chosen by Congregationalist ministers, sometimes within walking distance — as was the case with Olchon in the parish of Clodock and Rhydwilym in the parish of Llandysilio — of the borders of two or three counties where sanctuary could be reached. Even when the Second Conventicle Act closed the loophole, Dissenters still absconded to neighbouring counties by walking across moorlands or wading through rivers. Stephen Hughes's flock at Pencader and Llandysul worshipped in the legendary cave at Cwm Hwplyn, while Rees Prydderch's congregation assembled at Craig yr Widdon cave near Llandovery. In mid Cardiganshire Dissenters met secretly on Llanddewibrefi mountain, and in Cwmystwyth coloured cloths were hung on bushes by women in order to inform worshippers that the coast was clear. Since some meetings were broken up with unnecessary brutality, passions were inflamed: those employed to apprehend worshippers at a conventicle in Llangybi, Caernarfonshire, in 1676 were ambushed and badly beaten by Dissenters. Not every Dissenter chose to escape the wrath of authority.

Nimbleness and shrewdness served Dissenters well, too, in their attempts to discover and take advantage of flaws and anomalies in the penal code. Ministers regularly thumbed the *Statutes at Large* in search of loopholes. Philip Henry was more thoroughly acquainted with the minutiae of the penal legislation than most magistrates and he was even capable of querying the legality of the Five Mile Act. When Vavasor Powell was apprehended in October 1668 for allegedly addressing armed conventiclers in Merthyr Tydfil and was subsequently cross-examined by deputy lieutenants (some of whom were as drunk as lords) at Cowbridge and Cardiff, he relished the opportunity of pitting his wits against the authorities and publicly exhibiting his detailed knowledge of due processes of law. Even Quakers studied the law carefully, challenged the validity of writs, and explored the truthfulness of evidence presented in court. Peter Price, a prisoner at Presteigne under a writ of excommunication, spent hours mastering 'the good known Law of England' and pestered magistrates, lawyers and judges, only to be fobbed off with 'a parcel of self-justifying words'. Even those placed under lock and key for long periods were not all subjected to hideous brutalities. Well-disposed gaolers might grant them special favours, even to the extent of permitting them periods of parole to visit their families or fulfil long-standing preaching engagements. Whilst a prisoner at Welshpool, Richard Davies was allowed to embark on preaching tours, visit distressed Friends in Bristol, and discuss plans in London for emigration with William Penn.

There were brief but welcome respites from persecution which permitted greater freedom of manœuvre. One such interlude which enabled Dissenters to breathe more easily was the period between 15 March 1672 and 7 March 1673 when the penal laws were suspended. Initially, the Declaration of Indulgence was coolly received because anti-Roman Catholic legislation was also suspended. Dissenters nursed grave misgivings about accepting largess from a vain and unreliable monarch whose pro-Catholic and pro-French sympathies were manifest. [**DOCUMENT XXII**] The use of the royal prerogative also angered them. Many feared, too, that by registering the place of their meeting-houses they would invite closer surveillance and become vulnerable targets for further penal legislation in due course. In the event, however, most Dissenting ministers decided not to look a gift-horse in the mouth and duly applied for licences to conduct religious assemblies in private houses. A total of 185 preaching licences (136 in eight counties in south and mid Wales and 49 in five counties in north Wales) was issued, and twelve months of liberty enabled Dissenters to rally their forces and stiffen their resolve. A much more uncomfortable dilemma, however, presented itself when King James II, an avowed Catholic, issued a Declaration of Indulgence in April 1687 which afforded Dissenters a much greater degree of liberty than had been the case in 1672. On this occasion, Dissenters were not deceived by the Crown's extraordinary attempt to abuse the authority of Parliament and to bribe them by suspending the penal laws. Nor were they prepared to co-operate with the King when the Declaration was reissued on 27 April 1688. Indeed, there was much rejoicing in Wales when the trial and acquittal of the seven bishops prepared the way for the landing of William of Orange and subsequently the permanent toleration of Dissent.

One final consideration helped Dissenters to rise above their sufferings. The rigours of persecution were rendered much more bearable by alleged 'divine judgements' which befell informers, clergymen, constables, bailiffs and magistrates. Shortly after heartless bailiffs had robbed the Baptist Henry Gregory of his cattle, one of them drowned in a brook and another 'died miserably, eaten up by worms . . . like Herod'. David Maurice, a brutal Montgomeryshire magistrate, was thrown from his horse into the Tanat river and drowned. God's mercies also protected vulnerable Quakers. A clergyman who made off with a horse belonging to Frances Bowen, a Quaker widow from Llanfihangel, near Roggiet in Monmouthshire, and who swore loudly that he would not leave her with a groat, died ten days later. If persecutors were destroyed by the avenging hand of God, that same hand was also believed to be capable of intervening on behalf of steadfast witnesses for Dissent. Henry Maurice often told of how, during especially perilous journeys, he was 'hid in the hollow of God's hand'.

For all these reasons, persecution was not continuous or thoroughly unbearable, especially in the case of Congregationalists and Presbyterians, many of whom managed to establish a *modus vivendi* with local clergymen and magistrates. It is true that moderate men like Charles Edwards, Stephen Hughes and Peregrine Phillips spent short periods behind bars, that Philip Henry was robbed of possessions in lieu of a fine of £40 in the summer of 1681, and that many of their followers were forced to endure the psychological as well as economic effects of living 'under the Cross', but it cannot be denied that Baptists and Quakers bore the brunt of the persecution. The precise measure of injustice and brutality cannot be assessed statistically, but many instances of individual and collective suffering have been preserved in Dissenting annals which testify nobly to the fortitude and perseverance of radical non-conformists.

Baptists bore more than their share of heroic suffering during the years of persecution since they were still deemed capable of fomenting rebellion and undermining family life. The pejorative 'Anabaptist' label remained firmly pinned to their lapels and their activities continued to attract a good deal of publicity. Even after the prospect of continuous harassment and the lure of the New World had driven John Miles in 1663 to Massachusetts, where he helped to establish a Baptist church at Rehoboth and later the town of Swansey, his successors contrived to thrive on confrontation, disputes and dog-fights. Rumours that Baptists were heavily involved in plots and conspiracies were strengthened by reports that ministers who were interrogated by the authorities were prone to fits of absent-mindedness. A rash of violent attacks was loosed upon the most prominent activists. Henry Williams, a former disciple of Vavasor Powell, who kept a Baptist conventicle at Ysgafell in Llanllwchaearn, Montgomeryshire, encountered violence which scarred him for life. He spent long years in prison, his father was murdered, his wife cruelly maltreated, his house razed to the ground and his stock impounded. However, one field, which later became known as *Cae'r Fendith* (The Field of Blessing), was left untouched by his persecutors and duly produced what Williams's elegiast called 'an army of joyful corn' which saved his family from ruin. Told and retold by successive generations of Baptists, this story inevitably entered the annals of Dissenting hagiology and helped to stiffen the resolve of sufferers. As late as 1896, in his biography of Vavasor Powell, David Davies included a photograph of two stalks of the miraculous harvest at Ysgafell, which were the proud possession of a local farmer.

Baptist activities also evoked callous behaviour in neighbouring counties. Even the penury and misery of Henry Gregory, an Arminian Baptist who lived at Cwm, a small farm in the parish of Llanddewi Ystradenni, Radnorshire, were insufficient to soften the hearts of cruel bailiffs who robbed him of all his stock, even his last milking cow. In Breconshire, not even the deceased were afforded respect. When the body of a virtuous young Baptist woman was secretly buried at night in the churchyard of Llanfihangel Brynpabuan, the local incumbent furiously insisted that the body be dug up, dragged on a cart to a public crossroad and reburied after the manner of a common suicide or murderer. It is not hard to understand why a group of Arminian Baptists from Llanddewi Fach in Radnorshire fled to Philadelphia in September 1683. Those who had no wish to leave Wales for America were obliged to keep their heads down. No baptisms were recorded at Rhydwilym Baptist Church between December 1682 and December 1687, years when the Anglican backlash was at its most acute.

It was the Quakers, however, who were still the most widely loathed. Singled out for unusually harsh treatment, they, more than any other sectarians, were forced to bear 'the Burthen in the Heat of the Day'. Unlike most Dissenters, who deliberately avoided public confrontations with the ecclesiastical or secular authorities, Quakers openly flouted the penal code, thrived on public attention and made no effort to resist being arrested. From 1661 onwards, largely for pragmatic reasons, Quakers nailed their pacifist colours to the mast. In sermons and pamphlets they urged their enemies to beat their swords into ploughshares and their spears into pruning hooks. Their consciences would no longer permit them to bear arms and they were prepared to suffer passively as martyrs to the cause. Quakers believed that those who were actively engaged in the 'Lamb's War' were duty-bound to suffer. They braved all dangers, testified openly to the Spirit of the Lord and, no matter how often goaded or derided, accepted suffering without ever succumbing to bitterness or anger. Their enemies were often annoyed and bewildered by their non-violence. Non-Quakers were baffled when Elizabeth Lloyd of Dolobran, wife of Charles, voluntarily elected to join her husband in Welshpool gaol, leaving her son of four months in the hands of a nurse.

Although Quakers no longer sought to turn the world upside down by violent means, they still bore public witness to the powerful inward experience which had transformed their lives and practised patterns of behaviour which excited comment and hostility. Quaker meetings were regularly broken up by armed constables and members were manhandled, kicked, beaten, whipped and tossed into prisons where straw beds or bare floors, meagre rations, and hostile felons, who picked their pockets and stole their victuals, awaited them. 'No Cross, No Crown' was William Penn's injunction, and Quaker records abound with poignant tales of their trials and tribulations, all carefully recorded as a means of hardening the resolve of sufferers and inspiring their successors. Apart from the Quaker Act of 1662, Quakers were vulnerable to charges of vagrancy, *praemunire* (a fourteenth-century punishment which was used as an instrument of persecution), and failing to take the oaths of allegiance. James Picton, a former Puritan schoolmaster, was publicly humiliated in a pillory before being detained on a charge of *praemunire* for ten years in Carmarthen Castle and Haverfordwest gaol. Even the old were abominably treated. Anne Thomas, a blind octogenarian, was kept under lock and key in Presteigne prison in the early 1680s, whilst 'honest old' Peter Price, a former magistrate, continued to testify against tithes in prison at the age of eighty-six. Although only five Quakers died in prison during the years of the penal code, this tiny figure does not adequately represent the degree of physical and mental suffering endured by those who were incarcerated in stinking cells hardly fit for animals let alone humans. Deprived of fresh air and adequate food, long-term prisoners found that their health was so seriously impaired that they were never the same again.

There were also petty acts of malice to endure; none caught the headlines but they were carefully recorded by Quaker committees for mutual edification and support. An irate householder at Welshpool chained his Quaker son to a post and left him unattended on a frosty night. Ellinor Ellis of Penllyn, a poor woman dependent on the charity of fellow Quakers, was robbed of her bedclothes, apron, knitting and books. Rondl Davies, vicar of Meifod, cut off the inheritance of his daughter Prudence when she defied him by marrying the village blacksmith, who was a Quaker. When the pacifist Quaker Lewis James of Llangolman in Pembrokeshire refused to contribute a shilling towards the wages of the local muster master, the high constable seized his Bible which was worth 3s. 4d. The recurrent objection of Quakers to the 'ancient oppression of tithe' also needs to be borne in mind. Year after year Quakers stood in passive silence as bailiffs and constables distrained (in lieu of unpaid fines) cattle, sheep, oxen, horses, pigs, corn, hay, rye, wheat, farm and household implements, cheese, bedclothes, Bibles and books, all of which were ludicrously undervalued in order to render the fines all the more burdensome. In market towns in Pembrokeshire town criers were employed to invite people to buy goods distrained from local Quakers. Throughout years of petty, malicious and often violent harassment, Quakers continued to bear each adversity with steadfast witness and astonishing courage.

For a generation and more, Welsh Dissenters lived under the shadow of a repressive penal code which robbed them of religious liberty, imposed upon them painful sufferings, and excluded them from the universities, municipal administration and political life. That the majority of Dissenters did not yield in the face of these pressures says much for their courage, resilience and vitality. Not all leading Dissenting ministers of the second generation, however, survived to witness the significant measure of toleration achieved in 1689. Among those who perished before 'the new dawn' were two zealous apostles who had been a source of inspiration for the Congregationalist cause. Henry Maurice, 'Apostle of Breconshire', died, aged forty-eight, in July 1682. His elegiast described him thus:

> Heare lieth one of Abel's race
> Whom Caine did hunt from place to place.

In June 1688, Stephen Hughes, the widely acclaimed 'Apostle of Carmarthenshire', died, aged sixty-five, at his home in Swansea. But the other leading crusaders — Richard Davies, Charles Edwards, Philip Henry, John ap John, William Jones, Hugh Owen, James Owen and Rees Prydderch — lived to celebrate the liberties for which they had striven so valiantly.

# 6.    'The Lord's Free People'

In spite of the constraints imposed by the Clarendon Code, there was intense activity and vigour in Dissenting circles, so much so that champions of the established church feared that it was only a question of time before unmanageably large numbers would subscribe to their cause. More out of fear than curiosity, therefore, measures were taken to assess the relative strength of the movement. A word of caution must be sounded here. Counting heads was an unfashionable exercise in Stuart Wales and those who prepared returns did not possess the refined statistical techniques which we have come to expect in modern censuses. There are no truly reliable statistics, and those figures which are available constitute no more than crude estimates. Even so, if we combine the statistical evidence supplied by the returns of conventicles with fragmentary information from church and court records, it is possible to offer some tentative generalizations about the numerical strength and the social composition of Protestant Dissent in Wales.

Fearing that Dissenting causes were prospering rather than withering, Archbishop Gilbert Sheldon issued in June 1669 inquiries designed to assemble information regarding the size, location and leadership of their congregations. The returns are at best unreliable and at worst seriously deficient. (121) Returns for the diocese of St David's are missing, informers revealed a suspicious fondness for round figures, and it is more than likely that the true number of Dissenting worshippers was deliberately minimized. More reliable, though not without its lacunae and anomalies, is the ecclesiastical survey known as the Compton Census of 1676. (25, 32) The mastermind behind the census was Thomas Osborne, Earl of Danby, and it was administered by Henry Compton, Bishop of London and Provincial Dean. The census returns have been subjected to critical scrutiny by Thomas Richards and, more recently, by Anne Whiteman. The organizers of the census were anxious to compile statistics relating to the strength of Popish recusants and Protestant Dissenters in England

and Wales, and the returns were compiled by Anglican incumbents or their curates during April and May 1676. In spite of Thomas Richards's claims to the contrary, no concrete evidence exists to suggest that incumbents were pressurized by Archbishop Sheldon to provide returns which were less than truthful. Even so, it is probable that compilers of the returns underestimated the true numbers of Dissenters either because it was never absolutely clear to them what constituted a Dissenter or because they had no wish to provide Dissent with the oxygen of publicity. Whatever the truth may be, the returns are undoubtedly riddled with curious errors and omissions (there is no mention, for instance, of the powerful Dissenting church at Merthyr Tydfil) and they must be used with great caution.

None the less, the 1676 census does provide a general guide to the comparative strength of Dissent. It pin-points in particular those areas where Dissenters were strong, active and influential. According to Whiteman's interpretation of the returns, aggregate totals for the four Welsh dioceses were as follows:

Bangor (247)          St Asaph (463)
St David's (2,401)    Llandaff (905)

To these should be added around fifty-two Dissenters who dwelt in parishes in the diocese of Hereford, thus giving a total of 4,248 for Wales as a whole.

First of all, it is clear that Dissenters were a tiny minority. Since the population of Wales was around 371,000 in 1670, they constituted only 1.15 per cent of the total population. Even if their numbers had been absurdly underestimated in the census, it would be hard to claim that Dissent was championed by more than 6,000 people, or 1.6 per cent of the nation. Indeed, it was to remain very much a minority movement until the Calvinistic Methodists abandoned the established church in 1811. All the evidence suggests, too, that the overwhelming majority of parishes in north-west Wales had no recorded Dissent of any kind. The diocese of Bangor, where church livings were rather plumper and clergymen probably more efficient and popular than was the case in south Wales, was still the graveyard of Welsh Dissent. There were more Dissenters in the town of Swansea than in the whole of the diocese of Bangor. Support for Dissent was largely confined in the area to fragile Congregationalist cells in Llŷn and Eifionydd and more durable Quaker conventicles in the Bala-Dolgellau area. In north-east Wales, notably the deaneries of Bromfield and Yale, and Marchia — the traditional haunts of Cradock and Llwyd — Dissent was well established. The centre of gravity here was Wrexham and district, which housed over a third of the 643 Dissenters in the diocese of St Asaph, a tribute to the inspiring example of John Evans, a Congregationalist minister who had married Vavasor Powell's widow. Even though the numbers of Dissenters in the diocese of Llandaff were seriously underestimated, south-east Wales still remained fruitful soil for sowers of sectarian seeds. Dissent was strong in five out of six deaneries: Abergavenny (189), Chepstow (195), Groneath (118), Llandaff (180) and Newport (173). Yet the chief headquarters of Dissent was the large, sprawling and penurious diocese of St David's. There were more Dissenters in this see than in the whole of the other three dioceses. The twin fiefdoms were the archdeaconry of Brecon (1,361) and the archdeaconry of Carmarthen (597). Here, more than anywhere else, old Puritanism (sometimes in its most radical and subversive form) was very much alive and kicking.

In many ways, the geographical, social and economic structure of Wales determined the degree to which Dissent had made inroads. The sparsely populated and economically underdeveloped 'dark corners' of the north-west had scarcely been touched by either Puritanism or Dissent. Morgan Llwyd had often complained that 'the land of our nativitie is asleep'; nowhere was this more true than of isolated rural communities in the rugged uplands of Gwynedd. Conversely, Dissent prospered best in populous, busy and thriving urban centres, particularly along the borders and in south Wales. Welsh towns were still small by modern standards, but they were important centres for the distribution and sale of agricultural produce, they housed prosperous middling sorts, and fulfilled vital commercial and industrial functions. As we shall see, Dissent appealed to educated, bilingual people — often merchants, craftsmen and artisans — and, according to the 1676 census, the twin citadels in Wales were Wrexham (132) and Swansea (292). In the case of both towns the numbers were almost certainly underestimated. The most populous town in north Wales, Wrexham was a major focus of the woollen trade and a distributing centre for rural produce. Its radical tradition dated back to the days of Cradock and Llwyd, many of whose disciples were shopkeepers, craftsmen and artisans who had vainly sought to fan the millenarian flame before succumbing either to Quakerism or the more disciplined ministry of the Congregationalist John Evans. Swansea was also a busy and rapidly expanding trading and industrial town, boasting close links with Bristol and Ireland. It was a fashionable

centre and particularly receptive to outside influences. Dissenting
ministers spoke warmly of it as a 'city of refuge', partly because
powerful soldiers and civilian administrators like Major-General
Rowland Dawkin and Col. Philip Jones (before his retirement from
public life) afforded them considerable protection from their enemies,
and partly because clause III of the Five Mile Act was not applicable
in the case of Swansea because the borough was not entitled to elect
a representative to Parliament. Several notable ministers joined
Marmaduke Matthews, the ejected minister of St John's, Swansea, in
this 'godly Welsh Bristol'. Daniel Higgs came from Port Eynon,
Stephen Hughes from Carmarthen, Lewis Thomas from Newton
Nottage, and William Thomas from St Mary's in the Vale of
Glamorgan. It was of comfort to them, moreover, that Dissenters
exercised powerful influence in borough politics. Radical veterans of
the revolutionary times, many of whom still clung to their republican
titles, remained a force to be reckoned with in the administration of
the town of Swansea.

Yet it cannot be said that Dissent was strong only in urban communities. It clearly profited from flaws in the parochial structure of
the church in rural areas in the impecunious dioceses of Llandaff and
St David's, especially where lack of pastoral supervision and in-
frequent sermons prompted disgruntled church-goers to throw in
their lot with Dissent. Wherever there were large parishes where
people were poorly served by underpaid or non-resident or lazy
pastors, Dissenting conventicles were at hand to fulfil their spiritual
needs. Gains were achieved in frontier zones, between two dioceses
(the deanery of Gower, where 457 Dissenters were recorded in the
1676 returns, was located on the border between the diocese of
Llandaff and the diocese of St David's), and between two or three
counties. Striking geographical and agrarian contrasts within a county
sometimes held the key to Dissenting gains. In Glamorgan, for
instance, there was a marked social and economic division between
the prosperous Anglican gentry who dwelt in the low-lying, fertile
*Bro* (Vale) and who ensured that their tenants were docile and
deferential conformists, and the squires and freeholders of the
*Blaenau* (Upland) who inhabited inhospitably cold, wet, pastoral
communities and whose proverbial independence and even cussed-
ness enabled Roundhead zeal to merge with antinomian and atheistic
heresy during the revolutionary years. In the small and isolated
village of Merthyr Tydfil in upland Glamorgan, Capt. Harry William
Thomas, a monoglot Welsh-speaking firebrand, was reputedly

capable of attracting between 300 and 600 worshippers to his robust conventicle. Maladministration of church wealth and defective pastoral oversight also meant that Dissenters were unusually numerous in the archdeaconry of Brecon. Here, too, there was a tradition of independence among squires and hill-farmers. The gathered church at Llanigon profited enormously from the influence of disaffected squires like Thomas Gwyn of Pantycored (a former supporter of Vavasor Powell) and Charles Lloyd of Maes-llwch, who later donated the land on which Maesyronnen, the first Congregational meeting-house in Wales, was built. Rivers, too, constituted and determined frontier zones. The Teifi valley was a particularly significant frontier, for it was south of the River Teifi that the Baptists and Congregationalists of west Wales established their most flourishing and durable congregations. In south Carmarthenshire clusters of churches were established in a zone stretching westwards from the River Llwchwr to the banks of the Cleddau.

Clearly, then, social and economic factors were of critical importance. But Dissent also owed its growth to the preaching and pastoral gifts of energetic leaders. Dissenting ministers believed that the conversion of 'one poor sinner' was worth 'an age's preaching', and so they set themselves the task of travelling regularly on horseback to minister to their flocks in private homes, barns, hay-lofts, caves and cellars. Among the most indefatigable itinerants was Henry Maurice, a Caernarfonshire-born Anglican who resigned his church living in Shropshire and converted to Dissent in 1671. The hallmark of his ministry was fervent preaching and prayer. [**DOCUMENT XXIII**] His gathered church of Congregationalists and Baptists at Llanigon in Breconshire comprised seven preaching elders and four deacons, all of whom learnt much from their pastor's 'wonderful skill in unravelling the very thoughts and inward workings of men's hearts'. Distance was no object for this 'wrestling Jacob', and his zeal and commitment took him to secret locations in Glamorgan, Carmarthenshire and even his native Caernarfonshire. His fellow Congregationalist, Stephen Hughes, 'Apostle of Carmarthenshire', sacrificed his wealth and health in order to preach the Gospel and publish godly books. Winning souls was his chief priority and he used to preach with such fervour that his hearers were often reduced to tears. 'If we are damned', he often cried, 'then woe, woe that we ever were born.' Hughes's winsome personality and moderation enabled him to woo the 'sober part of the gentry', thereby enabling him to nurture promising young ministers and establish at least eight fledgeling churches in rural Carmarthenshire. Much to the frustration of Welsh bishops, dynamic preachers such as these revealed glaring deficiencies in the administrative and pastoral structure of the established church.

Although Presbyterianism had its spokesmen in Wales — notably the erudite classicist Samuel Jones, who established the first private academy for gifted young Dissenters at Brynllywarch in the parish of Llangynwyd in Glamorgan, and Philip Henry of Flintshire, the silenced Puritan minister and celebrated diarist — the most numerous and influential groups of Dissenters were the Congregationalists. Presbyterians believed in a parochial system whereby congregations were governed by presbyteries and synods, while Congregationalists championed the autonomy of the gathered church. During the years of the penal code, however, the boundaries between the terms 'Presbyterian' and 'Congregationalist' became blurred and it became well-nigh impossible to distinguish between them. Mixed congregations of Presbyterians, Congregationalists and Baptists, served by sprightly itinerant ministers, flourished.

Congregationalist ministers willingly took up the Cross in order to preserve the liberty and integrity of their churches. Life was a constant challenge for them; ''tis their Lot to be ill treated', observed James Owen. Since many of them were kept under close surveillance, it was not easy to maintain contact with their congregations. The problem was partly resolved by the creation of 'county churches' made up of a number of individual congregations. Such a polity certainly characterized Congregationalism in the counties of Brecon, Cardigan, Carmarthen, Merioneth and Montgomery during the years of persecution. The church at Cilgwyn, Cardiganshire, had eight branches, while in Merioneth the indefatigable Hugh Owen was obliged to minister to six meeting-places within a twenty-mile radius of his home at Bronclydwr. Elsewhere, too, the system brought out the best in determined evangelists.

Congregationalist worship was plain and straightforward. Worshippers recited or sang psalms, listened to prayers and sermons delivered extemporaneously by the minister, and took notes for use in subsequent discussions on the hearth. Communion was celebrated either weekly or monthly, and children were regularly catechized. Family worship was encouraged and much valuable informal instruction was carried out within the privacy of the home. The effective oversight of members also lay at the heart of their fellowship. The Presbyterian Philip Henry might have disliked the manner in which Congregationalists threatened to 'pluck up the hedge of Parish order', but he found their rigorous discipline and mutual love wholly admirable. Most of all, 'the Lord's free people' prized the inner workings of the Holy Spirit. The seminal role of the confession of experience was particularly highly cherished. Vavasor Powell described 'experience' as 'the inward sense and feeling of what is outwardly read and heard; and the spirituall and powerfull enjoyment of what is beleeved'. By stressing the regeneration of souls, effective discipline and liberty of conscience, Congregationalists kept the torch of freedom of worship alight.

Since the Congregational witness and life-style called for spiritual commitment, knowledge and discipline, the congregations did not comprise poor, illiterate or disinherited people. On the contrary, sturdy squires and industrious yeomen in rural communities and well-to-do members of the mercantile community in towns formed the backbone of the gathered churches. At the mother church of Llanfaches in 1669 there were 'many persons of good Estates being Counted Gent. & such as either were in Actuall Armes in the late Rebellion or held up under such', while in Walter Cradock's native parish of Llangwm the congregation included 'some men of competent parts and breeding' whose annual rents ranged from £30 to £500. The vigorous economic development of Swansea meant that Stephen Hughes and his colleagues were able to recruit merchants, tradesmen and craftsmen, while Peregrine Phillips drew his supporters from those employed in the textile trade in the prosperous market town of Haverfordwest as well as from relatively comfortable yeomen from surrounding parishes. Women, too, were prominent in Congregational assemblies and although they had no power to preach they were esteemed for their piety, prudence and 'good stock of knowledge'. Alicia Watkins of Llanigon was said to possess 'a sweet gracious spirit' and an insatiable appetite for sermons, while Jane Samuel, one of Stephen Hughes's disciples at Pencader, 'performed all ye Duties of Religion with Diligence & Delight. Praying, Reading, meditating etc. was her Dayly Employment.'

Had such members been poor, they would not have been able to meet the costs of a minister's stipend. Henry Maurice and David Penry of Llanedi might have been of gentry stock, but they still had families to maintain. Although Stephen Hughes was the son of an affluent silk-mercer from Carmarthen, he depended heavily on the financial resources of his Swansea-born wife and the largess of well-disposed gentlemen. Following his ejection from his living in 1662, Marmaduke Matthews of Swansea lived in abject poverty, but his genuine compassion for other underprivileged citizens touched the conscience of his family, friends and acquaintances who sustained him with gifts of food and money. John Evans of Wrexham was in such straitened circumstances following the revocation of the Declaration of Indulgence in 1673 that he sold many of his precious books and took up part-time tutoring in gentry households. For such men, the spirit of self-sacrifice and the joys of mutual fellowship which characterized Congregational assemblies did much to sustain morale.

It is more difficult to trace Baptist fortunes after the Restoration, partly, as Joshua Thomas pointed out, because their leaders were reluctant to keep records 'lest their writings should be found out and produced to witness against them'. There are no diaries or autobiographies which might have told us how Baptists struggled with their sins and doubts, and the content of the famous Rhydwilym church-book is tantalizingly unrevealing. The first Welsh book in defence of adult baptism was not published until 1694. Clearly, most Baptists kept their heads down and jealously guarded their privacy.

Initially, their affairs took a turn for the worse. The combative Jenkin Jones vanished from the scene either during or after his imprisonment, and the adversarial John Miles lost his nerve in 1663 and seized his opportunity of fleeing to America with some alacrity. The long-term consequences for the mother-church at Ilston were disastrous: not a single Baptist was recorded at Ilston in the 1676 census. Following Miles's departure to New England, his torch was taken up by the likes of Lewis Thomas of the Moor in Newton Nottage, Robert Morgan of Llandeilo Tal-y-bont and William Prichard of Abergavenny. The Baptist cause still flourished in places like Olchon, Llanigon, Llantrisant and Llanwenarth, and members were content to walk or ride considerable distances to worship in either mixed or exclusively Baptist conventicles. The most intriguing development, however, occurred much further west on the banks of the River Cleddau, where William Jones of Cilmaenllwyd established the celebrated church of Rhydwilym in the secluded parish of Llandysilio on the borders of Carmarthenshire and Pembrokeshire.

William Jones's life is shrouded in mystery. We cannot even tell when he was born or when he died. What can be said with absolute certainty is that his ministry left an indelible imprint on the fortunes of Welsh Baptists. Following his release from Carmarthen prison, he travelled in 1667 to Olchon to be baptized by immersion, before returning to south-west Wales to plant a new church in soil which had been heavily puritanized by Stephen Hughes, David Jones and

Peregrine Phillips. Jones faithfully clung to the canons cherished by John Miles — immersion, close communion and personal election, and the laying on of hands — but he was a more compassionate and popular man than his predecessor. At any rate, the fledgeling church was formally constituted by July 1668, some time before the Second Conventicle Act began to bite. William Jones's energy and will-power put new heart into the Baptists of west Wales and eighty-six members had enrolled by 1676. One bold recruit was baptized in the icy waters of the River Teifi on Boxing Day! When Rhydwilym celebrated its twenty-first birthday in 1689, there were 113 proud members in its congregation.

Even so, the Baptist cause was very much a minority movement confined to south Wales. Its growth proved modest and the total membership was no more than 550 by 1690. Appreciable increases in the ranks of Welsh Baptists did not occur until after 1775. Little work has been done on the social composition of General and Particular Baptists, but we know that they were generally poorer than Congregationalists and that they were unable to sustain a full-time ministry. Although Baptists could count gentlemen, merchants and tradesmen among their trusty supporters in anglicized market towns like Abergavenny and Brecon, their most affluent members seem to have either conformed or opted for a quiet life during the persecution. Conventiclers in the west were of relatively humble background and some were undeniably of 'the poorer sort'. At Rhydwilym, only John Evans of Llwyn-dŵr could legitimately sport the suffix 'gent.', even though Griffith Howell of Rushacre had sufficient means to provide the new mother-church with a burial ground. The overwhelming majority of members, drawn from nearly forty parishes in Pembrokeshire, Cardiganshire and Carmarthenshire, were people with only one hearth, mostly pious, sober-minded small farmers, cottagers and labourers. That their ministers had not received any formal education mattered little to them; the lively sermons, fervent prayers and warm fellowship which characterized Baptist worship were sufficiently and often irresistibly attractive.

Quakers, for their part, experienced mixed fortunes during the years of the penal code. In spite of the trials and tribulations they were forced to endure, appreciable gains were achieved until the early 1680s among sturdy squires, yeomen and craftsmen in the rural counties of Merioneth, Montgomery, Radnor and Pembroke and among middling groups in lively towns like Haverfordwest, Swansea and Wrexham. The rigours of persecution and fear of worldliness prompted them to rely heavily on the close-knit fellowship which bound together 'God's despised people'. Shorn of the ecstasy and bellicosity which had characterized their behaviour in the 1650s, they became increasingly quietist, peaceful and institutionalized. In tiny meeting-houses bearing magical names like Dolserau, Tyddyn-ygarreg, Llwyngwril, Dolobran and Pontymoil, they bore silent witness to the inner light and maintained their testimony against tithes. George Fox kept a tight rein on discipline by establishing a highly efficient administrative organization based on weekly, monthly and quarterly meetings, men's meetings and women's meetings, and (from 1682 onwards) a Welsh yearly meeting. But for this administrative structure, Welsh Quakerism might not have survived two decades of fierce persecution. Testimonies and sufferings were carefully recorded (invariably in English), as were matters relating to apprenticeships, marriages, wills and burial grounds. The Quakers' code of conduct required members to train children in godly conversation and the Scriptures, to forsake idle recreations and fashions, to marry in the Lord and never with 'the world's people', to be honest and fair, and to care for fellow brethren who were poor, infirm or elderly. [DOCUMENT XXIV] 'Lord! lead me in a plain path' was a familiar plea in Quaker diaries. In their daily dealings with others they placed a high premium on honesty, integrity and industriousness. All this was achieved against a background of harsh and repressive measures which left their bravest itinerants languishing with bloody noses and bruised bodies in overpopulated prisons and foul dungeons. Inevitably, persecution took its toll: it prevented their leaders from waging 'the Lamb's War' effectively and it deterred potential recruits from joining their ranks.

The Quaker cause, moreover, was sadly enfeebled by the consequences of large-scale emigration to the New World. In March 1681 William Penn received a royal charter granting him the province of Pennsylvania. Shortly afterwards, twelve leading Welsh Quakers were invited to London to lend support to the 'holy experiment' on which Penn was about to embark in his newly acquired colony. They learnt from Penn himself, as well as from a variety of beguiling promotional tracts, of the untold benefits which life in the New Utopia could confer on them: substantial acres of cheap and fruitful land, city lots in Philadelphia, peace and freedom of worship, and participation in government. Mesmerized by Penn's personal charm and lofty ideals, they took up the challenge. Sufficient capital was raised to purchase 30,000 acres of land in 'the Welsh Barony', the bulk of which was sold in small parcels to prospective emigrants, most of whom proved to be small gentlemen, yeomen, craftsmen and their families.

The cumulative effect of imprisonment, fines and ruinous forfeitures, coupled with the fear of renewed harassment after 1681, undoubtedly persuaded many Quakers to cross the Atlantic. Promises of material improvement and economic security beyond their wildest dreams were also major inducements. Thomas Ellis of Is Cregennan in Merioneth was convinced that the Lord had opened 'a door of mercy' to embattled Quakers. From 1660 onwards the growth of multiple landed estates had served to widen the gulf between powerful gentry families and lesser squires and freeholders. The latter, slipping inexorably down the social scale, discovered in Penn's manifesto an unparalleled opportunity of recouping some of their dignity and status. The benign climate, fertile soils and mellow comforts of Pennsylvania were likely to prove a more attractive and profitable investment than farming acidic, wet soil in rugged upland communities in Wales. In the event, some 2,000 individuals risked the hazards of a journey in small, rickety sailing vessels across the Atlantic during the period between 1682 and 1700. This is not the place to recount their fortunes in William Penn's New Jerusalem. Suffice it to say that the province was so deeply riven by internal problems that the Welsh settlers found it impossible to maintain their autonomy.

During the period from 1660 to 1689, Quakerism relied heavily, though not exclusively, on the support of relatively comfortable middling groups in both town and country. Securing the support of influential gentry families like the Lloyds of Dolobran and the Hanburys of Pontypool helped such groups to consolidate their gains and afforded them protection from the worst rigours of the penal statutes. Influential landowners were sometimes able to plead successfully with magistrates on behalf of detained Quakers and to urge gaolers to exercise restraint. The convincement in November 1662 of the well-born, Oxford-educated gentleman, Charles Lloyd of Dolobran, proved a major feather in the cap of Quaker evangelists, and the manner in which he defended the principles of liberty of conscience and shared prison cells with humble sufferers earned him enormous respect. But the backbone of Quaker conventicles in rural shires was the yeomanry. Conventiclers at Meifod in Montgomeryshire in 1669 were described as 'well horsed', and 31 per cent of the emigrants from Merioneth between 1682 and 1700 were sturdy yeoman farmers, many of whom were closely linked by ties of blood and ancestry. In the towns, anticlerical and anti-tithe agitation appealed to blacksmiths, coopers, feltmakers, flaxdressers, glovers, gunsmiths and weavers, dozens of whom regularly appeared before the quarter sessions and assizes for absenting themselves from church or for holding conventicles. William Bateman, a resolute Quaker conventicler at Haverfordwest, was a well-to-do mercer who invited merchants, retailers and yeomen to worship at his home. Bryan Sixsmith was a Wrexham draper who secretly distributed Quaker books, while William Bevan was a merchant who supported the Quakers of Swansea by providing them with land for a meeting-house and a burial ground. Among other energetic Quaker enthusiasts were Elisha Beadles, an apothecary at Pontypool, Richard Davies, the Welshpool feltmaker, and Francis Gawler, the Cardiff hatter. Nor should we forget those who did well for themselves by acquiring prosperous estates and influential political and judicial positions in Pennsylvania. Thomas Wynne, the former freeholder and barber-surgeon from Caerwys in Flintshire, served as Penn's personal physician and was elected Speaker of the Provincial Assembly in Pennsylvania, while Thomas Lloyd of Dolobran, a gifted physician, became chief executive of the colony in 1684.

By 1689, however, it was evident that persecution and emigration had so seriously depleted Quaker conventicles in Wales that they were a mere shadow of their former selves. [**DOCUMENT XXV**] Although leading Welsh Quakers put on a brave face in the annual epistles which they sent to London, the future was extremely bleak. The veteran crusader, Richard Davies, who had resisted the temptation to emigrate, poignantly referred to his brethren as 'the remnant'. Having lost so many followers — 'men of independence and backbone, men of vision and energy', as R.T. Jenkins called them — Quaker meetings lapsed into quietism, introspection and, in many cases, atrophy. Their numbers had declined so swiftly and dramatically that even the most bigoted Anglican clergymen could afford to ignore them. Still derided, but seldom persecuted after 1689, they withdrew into their tents. The most radical of sects in Cromwellian days had withered into impotence.

It is important to remember that during the years of persecution the boundaries between these denominations (save for the Quakers) were often blurred. Nor would it be right to claim that all good men were at loggerheads over matters relating to theology and rubrics. There were issues on which churchmen and Dissenters found common ground, notably their hatred of Rome, their loyalty to the Crown, and their anxiety to promote practical piety and good works. Prudent charitable work and literary activity also helped to remove barriers to mutual co-operation between Anglicans and Dissenters. One particularly striking example is the Welsh Trust (1674–81), which brought together men who were, theologically at least, poles apart. Assisted by influential Anglican bishops and Puritan merchants, Thomas Gouge, the ejected minister of St Sepulchre, London, began setting up charity schools and disseminating Welsh literature. Gouge worked in harness with Stephen Hughes, the compelling Dissenting preacher whose pastoral dedication and acute concern for the well-being of illiterate people had made him a legend in his own time. [DOCUMENT XXVI] Both men bore no malice against their persecutors, disregarded differences of creed and theology, and proved adept at bridging gaps between rival factions. While Gouge stumped the counties of Wales in search of funds, Hughes commissioned or prepared translations of English best-sellers and passed them on to Charles Edwards (author of *Y Ffydd Ddi-ffuant* (*The Sincere Faith*) 1677, one of the outstanding classics of Welsh literature), who advised on literary matters and corrected proofs. As well as a substantial edition of 8,000 Welsh Bibles, the Trust published a variety of translations of works by 'affectionate, practical' Puritan authors like Bayly, Baxter, Gouge and Perkins, books which denounced sin and immorality, dwelt on the brevity of life and the terrors of hell, and called for sincere repentance and a lively, saving faith — all themes which lay at the core of the Dissenting tradition. Stephen Hughes, too, not only produced the first Welsh translation of Bunyan's *The Pilgrim's Progress* in 1688 but was also responsible for editing and publishing five editions of Rees Prichard's enormously popular collection of catchy religious verses which he entitled *Canwyll y Cymry* (*The Welshmen's Candle*). Such works were widely disseminated among seekers after salvation and must have helped to instil the reading habit and foster independent thinking. Edmund Calamy believed strongly that the advance of Dissent in Wales was 'an effect of the increase of knowledge there'.

James II's extraordinarily brazen attempts in 1687–8 to advance the Roman Catholic faith by suspending the penal laws also served to drive Anglicans and Dissenters into one another's arms. Both groups recognized the alarming political and religious threat posed by a Papist monarch and, whilst conversing with James Owen in Oswestry in the summer of 1688, Bishop William Lloyd promised 'if ever we have it in our power again, to shew that we will treat you as

Brethren'. The world was beginning to change. Old antipathies towards Dissent had begun to soften and there was widespread rejoicing when William of Orange landed at Torbay on 5 November 1688. He entered London on 18 December and five days later James II fled in ignominy across the waters. 'He is raised', cried James Owen of King William III, 'by a singular Providence to be a Deliverer of oppressed Nations.'

Calmer times clearly lay ahead for Protestant Dissenters. On 24 May 1689 the Act of Toleration, a major milestone in the history of Dissent, was passed. Except in the case of Socinians, it made Protestant Dissent legal and finally admitted that those who did not conform to the liturgy of the established church could not be silenced or suppressed. However welcome the statute might have been, it was by no means as comprehensive a charter of religious liberty as Dissenters had hoped; indeed, it was hedged around with irritating restrictions. Dissenting meeting-houses required licences issued by bishops and doors were to remain unlocked during hours of worship. Dissenters were still required to swear an oath of loyalty to the Crown, pay tithes and church rates, and serve as churchwardens and parish overseers. Moreover, they were still excluded from political and civic life, and universities remained forbidden territory to them. Although the day remained far off when Dissenters could count themselves free and equal citizens, the very fact that the movement had survived and was now free to build its own chapels and prosper was a matter of considerable pride and satisfaction to its supporters. The Welsh Baptists at Rhydwilym joyfully celebrated the coming of toleration by preparing a roll-call of members, while the churchbook of the Congregationalists at Cilgwyn, Cardiganshire, contains the laconic entry: 'liberty of conscience was made legal'.

During the years of the penal code, supporters of church and state had cause to lament the growth of religious pluralism and to mock, despise and persecute dissidents who opted out of the established church. Dissenters were considered outsiders, deviants, subversives, constantly at odds with the government of the realm and not to be trusted. The majority of people had no desire to join them or imitate them. Indeed, as late as 1689, fewer than 2 per cent of the population had been won over to Dissent. To the bulk of the populace, Protestant Dissenters were quirky, irreverent, rhetorical, moralistic, self-righteous and stubborn men and women. For their part, Dissenters were determined to carry the banner of liberty of conscience, to face the storms of repression and persecution, and to fight for the right to worship in freedom. The spirituality, fellowship and contentment which they had discovered had made their lives worth living and their religion worth suffering for. This embattled élite exercised an influence far in excess of its numbers and in the long run it helped to create a more just and humane society. Even though Dissenters were convinced that providence favoured their cause, not even the most optimistic of them in 1689 would have dreamt that by 1851 Nonconformity would account for three-quarters of the worshippers in Wales.

# Illustrative Documents

## DOCUMENT I

*The charisma of William Wroth, elder statesman of Welsh Dissent, is revealed in this account by Edmund Jones (1702–93), Congregationalist minister at Pontypool.*

The Bishop blamed Mr Roth for not obeying the king and the bishops to read the book of sports, and for his preaching so much out of time, as he counted it and Mr Roth in answer in some of his speeches spoke to the following purpose with tears and crying. Souls are going to hell my Lord in their sins, should not we endeavour all the ways we can to save souls etc. so as to affect the bishop himself that he also wept but said to Mr Roth I shall lose my place for your sake, to which Mr Roth replied, no my Lord you shall not lose your place for my sake. I give up the Church do you place an Incumbent in it to have the profit; I only desire the favour to preach a sermon in it now and then gratis . . . He was in all respects a strong Christian, and a foundation stone in the great building of God in Wales. He dealt closely and faithfully in his public Ministry. would often ask questions as he went along. Being once at Park y fân near Carffily to Visit Sir Ed: Lewis and walking in the Garden, the Gardener offered him some flowers and took them and returned him Sixpence. he said, I hear you lead a Loose Life, to which the Gardener replied, yes God forgive me. but I have a good heart. Mr Roth said, come to hear me tomorrow. He did, and Mr Roth shewing the evil of the heart in the sermon afterwards asked him what he thought of his heart now. He answered that it was bad indeed, he did not think it was so bad, and afterward lived a better life.

(National Library of Wales MS 128C, f.76 a–b.)

## DOCUMENT II

*Although William Erbery's recollection of the spiritual fellowship at Llanfaches is tinged with emotion and nostalgia, his account rings true.*

For though separated Churches were before in England, yet the first Independent Church (according to the New-England pattern) was set up in Wales; where the Saints have out-lived their persecutors, as there they suffered and stood out all the times of persecution, when the proudest Pastors in England dared not to show their faces; but hid their heads in Holland . . .

For I will speak the truth without partiality; there were not more spiritual and suffering Saints in any part of English ground, as were in Wales; so self-denying, and dying to the world, yea so wise-hearted and knowing Christians; let all the English Counties about them testifie, and will tell, how many Saints from Somerset, Gloucester-shire, Hereford-shire, Radnor, Glamorgan-shire came in multitudes with delight to Lanvaghes.

What light, and labour in the Spirit was then? how heavenly minded? what holy language among them? what watching? what prayers night and day, in the way they went, in the work they did at their plow; everywhere in private, that Spirit of prayer and pureness of heart appeared, nothing of Ordinances was then mentioned, but with fear in themselves, and forcing others by the Spirit, from living in them: all was Spirit and life, the Saints in Wales then lookt for.

And 'twould be so still, but that they are enbondaged to their Pastors and Teachers, and which is worse, to the world, in which they gaine much, by pleasing men.

Ah pity pitty poor Wales! how are thy mighty fallen? but they are rising againe. England is yet too high, too stately, too proud, too full of pomp, and profit, and pleasure, to come down in the flesh, and to rise in the Spirit; though they can speak fine words: but Wales is a poor oppressed people, and despised also: Gentlemen and all are down already; there's Frize, & Flannen; there's Bread and Cheese, and an Oaten cake with runing water; Oh there's a place for Christ to come.

(William Erbery, *Apocrypha*, London, 1652, pp.7–9.)


# DOCUMENT III

*Ordinances issued in 1643 and 1644 permitted the removal of altar rails, the destruction of images, crosses and crucifixes, and prohibited the use of organs, fonts, roods and surplices. This account, written by a committed royalist, tells of one of Sir Thomas Myddelton's sorties into north-east Wales in 1643.*

Now if you desire to know what I find by my little experience in Britain of the behaviour of our zealots, I can do no less, (if no more) than confirm what you have often heard. All the honest and religious Clergy of Wales were fled to Conway and other safe places, till our landing set them at liberty; which was every whit as welcome and seasonable, and even more needful in this than the weakest part of the Kingdom, than Sir Simon Harcourt's coming into Ireland,[1] the joy of which you came in the nick to take notice of. All the orthodox clergy of Cheshire and Lancashire are either here or in Yorkshire, or in prison. They say, that they have lately seized upon some men that would not publish in their Churches, that we were Irish rebels. I myself coming into the Church of Hawarden the morning after they were there, found the Common prayer-book scattered up and down the Chancel; and some well-read man without doubt, conceiving that the Common-prayers had been in the beginning of a poor innocent old Church Bible, tore out almost all Genesis for failing, it stood so dangerously it was suspected to be malignant. In windows where there was oriental glass they broke in pieces only the faces; to be as frugal as they could; they left sometimes the whole bodies of painted Bishops, though in their rochets.[2] But if there was any thing in the language of the beast, though it was but an *hoc fecit*, or at worst *orate* etc. (and I but guess for I could not read it when it was gone) which had stood many years, and might many more without idolatory, that was dashed out. They had pulled down the rails about the table, and very honestly reared them to the wall: (it was well they were in a coal Country, where fewel was plentiful) and brought down the table into the midst of the Church. Some of our soldiers came and swore it stood not right, (alas! that we have no better reformation), and set it close to the East wall again. At Wrexham they say (I was not there) they did the like villany almost in all points, and broke in pieces one of the best pair of organs in the King's dominions: which Sir Thomas Middleton took for his proper pillage to make bullets of.

(*A Collection of Original Letters and Papers Concerning the Affairs of England*, ed. Thomas Carte, 2 vols., London, 1739, vol. 1, pp.32–3.)

1. Sir Simon Harcourt (1603–42) was governor of the city of Dublin.
2. A white surplice-like vestment worn by bishops.

## DOCUMENT IV

*Walter Cradock strongly believed in the right of Everyman to give an account of the faith within him: 'hath he the spirit, or no?' was the yardstick against which he measured a preacher of the Word.*

And let us not be so curious, or scrupulous, as to hinder people that they should not preach the Gospel. Suppose people have no degrees in the University, or it may be have not the knowledge of the tongues, (though that were to be wished) let us not pick quarrels with them to stop their mouthes, and to hinder the preaching of the Gospel. And let us not think so hardly in these dayes, of those men that God hath raised to preach the Gospel. It is strange you shall have your Pulpits ring, calling them Tub-preachers, and Tinkers, and Coblers. We should think better of them; Why? they are filled with good newes, and they goe and tell it to others. We doe so usually in other things, when we have good newes, we run to our friends, and neighbours, and comrades, and make it known.

This is an age wherein God comes and fills his people, with the glorious light of the Gospel, and poore wretches, they cannot chuse but speak what they have seen, and heard; therefore be not so captious, and furious. The Lord hath spoken, who can but prophesie? Amos 3.8. When God fills peoples souls with the knowledge of Christ; who can keep it in? It is as the new wine spoken of in Job, it cannot be kept in. And surely the time is comming that young men shall see visions, and old men shall dreame dreames, and God will poure out his Spirit upon all flesh, and they shall prophesie; It is prophesied in Joel, and this is to be made good in the new Testament. And therefore if wee see that the Lord fills young men, or tradesmen, etc. and gives them hearts to go, and tell the good newes to others; why should you be so extreamely troubled, and spend your spirits in rage at it?

I use not to tell stories, but let me tell you this one thing; since I have been from you of late, I have observed, and seen, in the Mountaines of Wales, the most glorious work that I ever saw in England, unlesse it were in London; the Gospel is run over the Mountaines between Brecknockshire, and Monmouthshire, as the fire in the thatch; and who should doe this? They have no Ministers: but some of the wisest say, there are about 800 godly people, and they goe from one to another. They have no Ministers, it is true, if they had, they would honour them, and blesse God for them; and shall we raile at such, and say they are Tub-Preachers, and they were never at the

University? Let us fall downe, and honour God; what if God will honour himself that way: They are filled with good newes, and they tell it to others.

(Walter Cradock, *Glad Tydings from Heaven; To The Worst of Sinners on Earth*, London, 1648, pp.49–50.)

## DOCUMENT V

'*No King but Jesus' was the cry of the Fifth Monarchists, and Morgan Llwyd's poems in the 1640s were shot through with millennial expectations.*

lord wee are fruitlesse dull and weake
    and sinfull every way
now fill us full with Jesus Christ
    that honour him wee may.

lett our soules flourish with thy saincts
    in light in life and love
lett no corruption conquer us
    relieve us from above.

lord overthrow the Antichrist
    thine ancient people call
then lett thy glory fill the earth
    Unite thy people all.

lett Jesus Christ thy son our King
    bee ruler in our lands
lett Kings submitt & princes bow
    as with thy wisedome stands.

O lett his saincts be knitt in love
    his gospell preached bee
lord bring in many to thy selfe
    & so rejoyce shall wee.

And lord lett us that sing this song
    who have seene much of thee
already working in our dayes
    thy glory live to see.

(*Gweithiau Morgan Llwyd o Wynedd*, ed. T.E. Ellis, vol. 1, Bangor, 1899, p.33.)

# DOCUMENT VI

*A well-organized campaign, led by Alexander Griffith, sought to discredit the work of the propagationists.*

The great Cabal of the Itinerants instruction was to render the Ministers persons odious, and their Calling in its very basis to be Anti christian, and so in it self unlawfull and uselesse, and none to be protected or Countenanced by the Civil Magistrate. This without any greater Engin was instrumental enough to batter and eject them out of their Freeholds and Being, without any respect either to their fidelity and ability in their Teachings, or sobriety in their Conversations. And in what a narrow streight they were, either to be wholly deprived of all subsistence for the maintenance of themselves and Families, or turn Apostataes to their Ordination, we leave to that most ingenuous and modest Censure of a Noble Member of the House, in his Answer to a Narrative of the Cause and manner of the Dissolution of the last Parliament.[1]

Though he and the Itinerants cryed down Tithes as Mosaical Ceremonies and Anti-Christian, yet he and they, or such as are their Agents, have had the disposing of above Forty Thousand pounds a year in Tithes, Gleabs, impropriations, Rents reserved, and other ecclesiastical benefices and promotions, far above four years last past in the thirteen Counties of Wales, far surmounting the sum of One Hundred and Threescore Thousand pounds, and as yet to our knowledge unaccounted for, and what account is given to the State for the Tenths, since the Act of Propagation of all ecclesiastical promotions in Wales, we refer to the better knowledge of that worthy Gent. Mr. Baker, Master of the first fruits Office.[2]

That notwithstanding all this great Revenue by them received, there are above seven hundred Parishes in the thirteen Counties unsupplied with any Ministers, who (we are confident) dare own the charge, and you may ride ten or twenty miles on the Lords day, where there is twenty Churches, and not one door opened, and for most of the Itinerants, they are such ignorant persons, that they can neither read, nor understand English, nay some of them more scandalous than any of the ejected Ministers, and all of them in their Principles and Doctrines destructive to Government.

(Alexander Griffith, *Strena Vavasoriensis, A New-Years-Gift For The Welch Itinerants, Or a Hue and Cry after Mr Vavasor Powell*, London, 1654, pp.4–5.)

1. *An Answer to a Paper entituled A True Narrative of the cause and manner of the Dissolution of the late Parliament* (1653) was published on the occasion of the dissolution of Barebone's Parliament in December 1653.
2. Thomas Baker, deputy remembrancer of the First Fruits Office.


# DOCUMENT VII


*No Puritan saint preached the Gospel with greater zeal than 'the Metropolitan of the Itinerants', Vavasor Powell.*


. . . he was called into Wales again, where he renewed his former labours preaching the Word in season and out of season, so that by him Christ made manifest the favor of his knowledge and grace in every place throughout the Country, insomuch that there was but few (if any) of the Churches, Chappels, Town halls in Wales wherein he did not preach Christ. Yea very often upon Mountains, and very frequent in Fairs, and Markets, it was admirable to consider how industrious he was by his often preaching in two or three places a day, and seldome two dayes in a week throughout the year out of the Pulpit, nay he would sometimes ride a hundred miles in a week, and Preach in every place where he might have admission both day and night, if he passed through any Fair, or Market, or near any great concourse of People (so great was his love to Souls) he would take the opportunity in his Journey to preach Christ, yea his whole life was a continual preaching, giving seasonable instruction to every body he met with being fruitful and exemplary in Word, Doctrine, Conversation, Spirit, it was his custome where ever he came to leave some spiritual instructions and gracious favour behind him.

He was imbued with such courage of mind & furnished with such ability of body that he went through his work with great delight, many admiring how he was able to hold out, he was an able Minister of the new Testament, and always in readiness upon all occasions to fulfil his Ministry, and like the good Householder brought forth of his Treasury, things new and old, being very indefatigable in his work, speaking and praying sometimes, 3.4. nay 6, and 7. hours together.

(Edward Bagshaw, *The Life and Death of Mr Vavasor Powell*, London, 1671, pp.107–8.)

## DOCUMENT VIII

*Henry Vaughan, 'Silurist', the greatest Anglo-Welsh poet of the seven-teenth century, believed that Puritan saints were poisoning the minds and hearts of Welsh parishioners.*

A Prayer in time of persecution and Heresie

Most glorious and Immortall God, the Prince of peace, unity and order, which makest men to be of one mind in a house, heale I beseech thee these present sad breaches and distractions! Consider, O Lord, the teares of thy Spouse which are daily upon her cheeks, whose adversaries are grown mighty, and her enemies prosper. The wayes of Zion do mourne, our beautiful gates are shut up, and the Comforter that should relieve our souls is gone far from us. Thy Service and thy Sabbaths, thy own sacred Institutions and the pledges of thy love are denied unto us; Thy Ministers are trodden down, and the basest of the people are set up in thy holy place. O Lord holy and just! behold and consider, and have mercy upon us, for thy own names sake, for thy promise sake suffer not the gates of hell to prevaile against us; but return and restore us, that joy and gladnesse may be heard in our dwellings, and the voyce of the Turtle in all our land. Arise O God, and let thine enemies be scattered, and let those that hate thee flee before thee. Behold, the robbers are come into thy Sanctuary, and the persecuters are within thy walls. We drink our own waters for money, and our wood is sold unto us. Our necks are under persecution, we labour and have no rest. Yea, thine own Inheritance is given to strangers, and thine own portion unto aliens. Wherefore dost thou forget us for ever, and forsake us for long a time? Turne thou us unto thee, O Lord, and we shall be turned, renew our dayes as of old. Lord hear, and have mercy, and be jealous for the beloved of thine own bosome, for thy truth, and for the words of thine own mouth. Help us, O God of our salvation, and for thine own honours sake deal Comfortably with us, Amen, Amen.

(*The Works of Henry Vaughan*, ed. L.C. Martin, 2nd ed., Oxford, 1957, p.166.)

## DOCUMENT IX

*By 1652 William Erbery had become not only a passionate opponent of tithes but a fierce critic of adventurers and careerists who used the propagation for their own private gains.*

Then the oppression of Tithes came to my ears, and the cry of the oppressed filled my heart, telling me, That I and my children fed on their flesh, that we drunk their blood, and lived softly on their hard labour and sweat.

All the Petitions against Tithes were presently presented and spread before me by God, who asked, Is it not the gain of oppression that thou and thine live on?

Truly Sir, there was never a day went over my head, but I heard something of him from God, and from men also, who, not knowing the working and wrath that was within, did continually hit me in the teeth with something of Tithes.

One came to my Chamber, a worthy Gentleman from England, complaining of the Commissioners of Monmouth-shire, who (as he came along) had a meeting at Christ-Church, to take a more strict account of each mans Tithes, and that he met with many poor Country-men in the way crying out of their oppression, and that (as they said) by the people of God.

Another day an honest man of our Country, comes in and tells me, he had formerly taken a good bargain of Tithes, from the Commissioners of Glamorgan-shire, but he had no rest in his Spirit from the time he farmed it from them, but was continually tormented till he delivered it up, which he did (as he said) very quickly, else he thought in his heart he had run stark mad out of his wits.

And truly Sir, 'twas so with me in this, though I have been afflicted from my youth, and suffered the terrors of the Lord to distraction; yet (for the time) I was never so distracted, confounded, and filled with fears in all my former temptations, as in this of Tithes.

And yet this trouble was not like those legal terrors I suffered of old; but it was like fire in my bones, which I believe is the eternal Spirit, and everlasting burnings, which will shortly break forth upon all the oppressors of the land, to burn up their flesh, fulness, and those fair buildings which they have raised on the ruines of others, enrichings themselves in the Nation's poverty.

(William Erbery, 'The Grand Oppressor, Or, The Terror of Tithes; First Felt, and now Confest. The Sum of a Letter, written to one of the Commissioners in South Wales, April 19, 1652.' *The Testimony of William Erbery*, London, 1658, pp.50–1.)

# DOCUMENT X

*Llyfr y Tri Aderyn (1653), by Morgan Llwyd, was a warning to the Welsh to prepare themselves for the imminent return of Christ. In the following passage, the Dove, representing the Puritan saints, expresses Llwyd's social radicalism and also movingly describes his spiritual pilgrimage.*

But woe unto you, lawyers, there is a law that will consume you. Woe to the contentious in a land, firebrands of hell be they. Woe unto you physicians — murderers — many a groan hath gone up to the other shore against you. Woe unto you, oppressors, who swallow down riches; ye shall vomit them all up again together with your own life-blood. Woe unto you, high and mighty ones, evil in your example, who drag down after you the poor to their destruction; how shall you give an account of your wretched tenantry? What will become of you when everything lofty shall be broken and consumed with fire. Woe to every tree, great and small, that bringeth not forth good fruit; the fire hath been kindled in Wales and the entrance to the forest (O! land of modern Britons) is open wide to the fiercely burning fire; and the axe, too, is at thy root — unless thou forthwith bearest good fruit, thou shalt be cut off from being a people . . . Woe unto you who come together where crowds collect, gay of spirits, eating the sweets of the lust of the flesh in the devil's daily round, and spending your lives in carousal; shortly there will not be a drop of water to be had to cool the tip of your tongues. Woe unto you, gentry, who lick up the very sweat of the poor, causing your tenants to groan and crushing their very bones; the time of your own crushing hasteth and delayeth not. Woe unto you, dumb clergy, who show affection for the foxes, and snarl at the sheep: blind dogs, bitter, proud, idle, greedy, growling, sleepy, coarse, and foul, ye shall all be sent adrift out of the Church. And woe to you all, Welshmen in years, who are still unchanged. But blessed are ye who long after God, ye shall be filled with Him, in Him, and for Him.

. . . I was, by nature, dead, and when I realised that, I had a desire to live, but I could not do so till everything in me and around me was dead to me; and then, forthwith the Creature lost its hold upon me, and in that instant I got a hold on the Creator, or rather, He laid hold on me. Previously, I had heard sermons, but I did not listen to them; I sung Psalms, but my heart was dumb; I took the sacrament, but I saw not the body of the Lord. I discoursed about, and said, many a thing, but not from my heart, in all truthfulness, till the rose budded forth in me. And after all the commotion, I was forced to end everything at last before I could begin, and die before the grain of wheat could shoot through my soil.

. . . Look momentarily for the Day of Judgment, seek peace, love the truth, and the God of all true peace will be with thee and in thee. But, and if thou wilt not act up to this, my advice, but refusest to hear my voice, behold! a rotting carcase wilt thou become in the land, and a tormented prisoner in the bottomless pit with never a hope of changing thy lot. But, O! thou winged Eagle, I have an idea that thou art ripe for goodness; therefore, it is my heart's desire that thou, too, shouldst fly away throughout the thirteen counties of Wales and tell them in every town and village, in every parish and hamlet, in every neighbourhood and family, to every branch of Adam, old and young: — Repent; the Kingdom of the Great King is at hand.

> (Morgan Llwyd, *Llyfr y Tri Aderyn* [*The Book of the Three Birds*], London, 1653. Transl. by L.J. Parry in *Transactions of the National Eisteddfod of Wales*, Llandudno, 1896, pp.251, 252, 268, 273.)

## DOCUMENT XI

*Vavasor Powell doggedly refused to accept that the millennial cause was in ruins, and in a letter to Cromwell which prefaced* A Word for God *(1655) he denounced the 'villainous' Protector.*

Sir, For as much as you have caused great searching of heart, and divisions among many of God's people by a sudden, strange, and unexpected alteration of government, and other actions, to the great astonishment of those, who knew your former publick resolutions and declarations; considering also, how (contrary to foregoing acts and engagements) you have taken upon you a power, by which you are utterly disinabled (if there were in you a heart) to prosecute the good things covenanted and contended for, with so many great hazards, and the effusion of so much blood; and by reason whereof you are become justly suspected in your ends in time past, and actions for future, to very many of those, of whose affections and faithful services you have enjoyed no small share, in all the difficult passages, and enterprizes of the late war.[1] These things considered by us, (as we know they are by many churches and saints) and there being a deep sense upon our spirits of the odium under which the name of Christ, his cause, people, and ways do lie (as it were) buried; and also of the exceeding contempt, which the wonderful and excellent operations of God are brought into, even those eminent wonders, which the nations have been spectators and witnesses of, and wherein your hands have been partly engaged; we cannot, after much serious consideration and seeking of the Lord, many of us, both together and apart, but present to your hands the ensuing testimony, which (however you may look thereon) is no more than necessity exacts from us, for the clearing of our own souls from guilt, and discharging of our duty to God and men. Therefore we earnestly wish you to peruse it and weigh it, as in the sight of God, with a calm and Christian-like spirit; and harden not your neck against the truth, as you will answer it to their great judge, before whose impartial tribunal you (as well as we) shall be very shortly cited to give an account of the things done in the body, whether good or evil. Where the true motives and ends of all your actions will be evident, where no apology will be accepted of your slighting and blaspheming of the spirit of God, nor for the hard measure you give his people, by reproaches, imprisonment, and other oppressions; and where pride, luxury, lasciviousness, changing of principles, and forsaking of good ways, justice and holiness will not have the smallest rag of pretence to hide them from the eyes of the judge, which things (whatsoever you say for your self) are (even at present) to be read in your forehead, and have produced most sad effects every where. Especially first, the filling of the saints hearts and faces with inexpressible grief and shame. And secondly, the stopping (at least) of the strong current of their prayers, which was once for you, if not the turning thereof directly against you. To these we might add (thirdly) the hardening of wicked men, yea the refreshing and justifying of them in their evil doings, and speaking against the gospel, name, and spirit of our Lord Jesus Christ. And lastly, God's signal withdrawing from you his designs. Oh, then! that you would lie down in the dust, and acknowledge your iniquity, and return unto the Lord by unfeigned repentance, doing your first works; and that you would make hast to do so, lest God's fury break forth like fire upon you, and there be no quenching of it. This would rejoice us much, as being real well wishers to your soul's everlasting happiness, though we must declare with equal piety and detestation against your designs and way.

(*A Collection of the State Papers of John Thurloe*, ed. Thomas Birch, 7 vols., London, 1742, vol.4, pp.380–4.)

1. I.e., the civil wars, 1642–8.

## DOCUMENT XII

*In this poignant letter, dated 27 June 1659, Vavasor Powell sought to repair relations with his former ally, Morgan Llwyd. Alas, Llwyd had died on 3 June.*

My very deare friend & brother.

The auncient affection is not extinguished, & I hope rather encreaseing & renueing then decayeing, tho. I cannot iustifie my neglect in visitting you soe long, tho ther were divers things hindered, as my owne frequent, & continued infirmities, my being from home, hearing of your Recovery wn I once intended to come, together wth some other Rea: better suprst than exprst. I hope wtever fire was kindled (beside zeale for our owne Judgemts) god hath in some measure quenched it, & our Lord's visitat: hath cooled or spirits, that if we have ye happines to see one another againe 'twilbe without any animosity, priudice, or evill surmise wch hath beene too long gendred in ye hearts of ye Sts. one agt another. I hope if I have given you any offence to heare, acknowledge & satisfie, I doubt not of ye like from you: my lines would have signified ye continuance of my love, had I suppos'd they would have beene welcome. however I can say in the sight of ye Ld. I never unsainted you in my opinion, nor unfriended you in my desires. You were never out of my heart, nor shut out of my poore prayers: & I finde an honest intention to doe wt in me lies to remove all ground of disaffection, & Spirit: comunion. If I know my self, you may commit as much trust in me as ever you could, or as in another St. of equall infirmities, & temptacons. If I come to Wrex: shortly, iudge it is ptly, (yea chieffely) to visit you & not to divide, as some have formerly (ye Lord lay it not to their chardge) thought & spoken. Brother I cannot adde, but that I am truly, & I hope sencibly affected wth yor manifold afflictions: wishing (as to myself in qualitie & degree) a sanctified issue thereof, & wherein I may serve ye Lord for you, or you in, & for him,

Yor once credited, & still to be beleeved (brother) friend.

Va: Powell

27th of ye 4th Mon. 59

(National Library of Wales MS 11439D, f. 32.)

# DOCUMENT XIII

*The following rules and regulations were agreed at a meeting of Baptist members at Ilston on 16 October 1650.*

The Church, taking Into serious Consideration the great distance of most of the brethren and sisters one from another and other things that will hinder them from meeting together In one place as oft as wee could desire dureing this winter season, together wth the great and apparent Inconveniences that would necessarily follow If frequent meetings were not held up, and Continued doe wth one Consent declare and Order That the whole Church shall meet once in three weeks at Ilston upon the ffirst day of the week to break bread together, And that on the other 2 first dayes of the sayd 3 weeks, they are to meet In three sevrall places; (that is to say) our brethren and sisters in the west. pts of Gower at Landewi, those neere Ilston at Ilston, and those Inhabiting in Carmarthenshire and other Welsh pts at sister Jennet Jones howse[1] or elsewhere thereabouts where they shall see most convenient.

And that in the midle of evry week there shall bee the Like sevrall meetings in the sayd sevrall places (that is to say) In the Welsh pts on the third day of evry week; at Ilston on the ffowrth, And at Landewi on the ffift; And that the brethren at evry of these meetings shall Constantly enquire Concerning the Condition and Conversation of evry of the brethren and sisters Living neere them and take especiall Care to Counsell admonish exhort and faythfully to reprove one another, and to recomend any such businesse to ye Church when they shall see Cause.

And therefore It is ordered agreed upon and decreed that from this day forward the whole Church are to meet together at Ilston, to heare and determine all such businesses as shall bee presented before them once in three weeks upon the 4th day In the morning.

The Church humbly Considering theyr present weaknesse and want of guifted men to prophecy, doe desire bro: Myles[2] and bro. Proud[3] to take especiall Care to preach at all the Church Meetings that shall bee held before the world. And doe further order that, upon that ffowrth day wch hath been apointed to bee once In 3 weeks fore the ordering of Church affayrs, there shall bee two or more brethren desired by the church to exercise theyr guifts in private before the Church in the morning; provided that noe brethren bee hindered to speak when the Lord shall Imediatly move thereunto.

And to the end that there may be alwayes a publick ministery kept up by this Church at the place of theyr more Constant & frequent meetings where the Lord first began his work among them and gathered them together; and that they might bee as a golden Candlestick holding forth Light and trueth in this dark place, they have thought fit to order that there shall bee Constant preaching at the publick meeting howse at Ilston evry ffirst day of the week in the aforenoon: and to that end doe desire brother Myles or some other bro. by his procuremt to bee hence forward two ffirst dayes of evry three weeks and brother Proud to bee ye third preaching publickly there.

(National Library of Wales MS 9108D, f. 12.)

1. Weekly Baptist services were held at Jennett Jones's house at Berwig in Bynea, near Llanelli.
2. John Miles, founder of the Baptist church at Ilston.
3 Thomas Proud was John Miles's right-hand man at Ilston.

## DOCUMENT XIV

*This pamphlet attempted to expose the alleged 'unjust, Barbarous, Inhumane, Trayterous practices' of 'Anabaptists', led by Capt. Jenkin Jones of Llanddeti and his armed followers.*

[Corporations] have preserved their Liberty, and defended Society in an eminent manner: Together with their Forms and Customs, which, with very little alteration, will consist and fit with the Form of the best Constituted Commonwealth that can be thought of: these People are not against the Form, but their aym is at the Power, and when they cannot attain that, then they destroy the Form to come at the Substance: They cry down the Lawes and Customs as Corrupt, that they may Govern by no other Laws then their Lusts, Ambition, and Ignorance: By this example, the People of England may be forewarned of the ensuing dangers that will inevitably befall London, and other Corporations in the Nation; the preventing of which, together with the many other Invasions of Rights and Liberties, threatened by these Levellers, who, under a pretence to get Arms into their Hands, to secure the Interest of the good People, will Ruine, Destroy, and threw down all that we have to defend our Lives, Liberty, and Estates; and instead thereof Erect a Righteous Government, after the mode of John of Leyden, and Knipperdolling.[1] Who had Commission and

Call, as they pretended, from God, to kill all the wicked Kings, Magistrates, and People, that the Saints might possesse the Earth; that is to say, all those that are not of their perswasion. This Design of the Anabaptists here, hath bin carryed on under-hand this ten years and more by their Confederates; they have obtained a great part of the Places of Trust and Profit in the three Nations; by which means there hath bin a Seminary of Hypocrites created, Men fit to ayd in any Change of Government, and the Effecting of any Villainy whatsoever. These People's design doth extend yet further, that is to say, not onely to destroy the Ministry, but also the Magistracy, that none may be left to preserve publick Interest.

(*An Alarum to Corporations: Or, The Giddy sort of Hereticks Designs, unmaskt,* London, 1659, p.8.)

1. Jan Bockelson (1510–36); Bernard Knipperdolling. They were twin leaders of Anabaptist refugees who attempted to establish a kingdom of saints in Münster in 1533–4.


# DOCUMENT XV

*Thomas Wynne's account of his quest for truth; the searing inward experience which transformed his life is remarkably vivid.*

I was Baptized and brought up a Protestant, and having learned the Articles of their Faith, and the Prayer of the Church, I thought all was well, untill I was about fifteen Years old, and then soon after it happened that I could not find any such Church as I was baptized into; the Wolf was got among them, who tore many of them to pieces, and the rest fled: So that go to what Church I would, I could find neither Bishop, Doctor, Prebend, Vicar nor Curat, to look after my Soul (viz.) not one of my Protestant Instructers, they were all fled and left me to the mercy of the Wolf that had worried them; and for many Years together there were none of them so much as visited me, nor sent me so much as an Epistle or Collect, nor any comfort or hopes.

But before I was twenty Years of Age I was amazed and astonished to see what was come to pass, and began to reflect upon my self, and to think what would become of my poor Soul, For those who pretended to be my guides to Heaven were fled, & I knew not the way. And my Brethren the Protestants without any more ado, both great & small, went to hear the Hirelings that were then set up, unless it were here there one, and most of these men of low degree, such as they could get nothing off; and when I saw it thus come to pass, I went also for company, but found their great matter was to Exclaim against the Protestants, which hit me upon the Sore . . . by this time I began to question whether any were then to be found in the right or not: For my Instructers were fled, and the others at best were but miserable Comforters; for turn to the Right hand or Left I saw Iniquity abound, and then I began to recollect my self, and consider what my God-Fathers and God-Mothers (so called) had promised and vowed for me in my Baptism, as they called it, (viz.) That I should forsake the Devil and all his Works, the Pomps and Vanities of this wicked World, and all the sinful Lusts of the Flesh: This indeed was to forsake all Sin; but how to perform I could not tell, for I had lost my Guides that so taught.

. . . then began my Sorrow to encrease, and to be more than I could bear; and this was the time, dear Country-men, that the Almighty God, who is no Respecter of Persons, did break in upon my Soul by his Everlasting Light . . . [I] can do no less then give in my Testimony concerning the Operation or Working of the Heavenly Power, it wounded as a Sword, it smote like a Hammer at the wholy Body of Sin, & in my Bowels it burned like Fire, yea, so dreadfully it burned, that it made my Bowels boyl, it pierced as a Sword, it broke as a Hammer: And then the Pangs of Death I felt in my Members which did make me to roar, yea, and to Quake and Tremble: for this Fire, when it burned, it gave Light, as its the Nature of Fire to do, and it discovered to me and these poor despised People the great body of Sin and Death, which was indeed terrible to behold.

(Thomas Wynne, An Antichristian Conspiracy Detected, London, 1679, pp.8–10.)

## DOCUMENT XVI

*One of the 'Valiant Sixty', the Quaker Thomas Briggs, a native of Bolton-le-Sands, Lancashire, incurred the wrath of the Welsh for his stubborn and provocative behaviour. Was he the first 'streaker' ever seen on the streets of Cardiff?*

And it was upon me to go through most part of Wales to declare the mighty, and terrible day of the Lord God of power; and in a Town called Clanzous,[1] as I was so declaring, many People were attentive a pretty time, till the Constable came forth and stirred up the People, and Cryed out, Kill him, Kill him; and they did throw stones upon me that were so great, that I did admire they did not kill us; but so mighty was the power of the Lord, that they were as a Nut or a Bean to my thinking. The Constable himself took hold upon my Coat, with an intent to have pulled me down under his Feet; and my Coat did Rent: and he got the one half, and the other did hang about my Neck, and one that was with me, said, let us flee for our Lives; and it rose up in me, that I might fight the Lords Battle and not flee. And I turned again upon him in the dread of the Lord, you must give an account for this daies work; and one Man came with the half of my Coat, and desired me to take it again, for he was smitten inwardly, for that which they had done; and I put off the other part that was about my Neck, and left it with them, to be a Witness against them, and afterward they sowed it together and sent it to a Friends House. I was moved of the Lord to go through Cardiff for a sign, I got up in the Morning, and went out of a Friends House, with my Coat upon me till I came into the Street, and when I came there, I let my Coat fall down, and so went naked up and down through the Streets; and this was the Message that the Lord put into my Mouth, to declare unto them, which was a Town of great Profession; Thus must you be stripped of all your Profession, that are not found in the Life of Righteousness: and I went through a Steeple-House where People were gathered to Worship, and the power and dread of the Lord God that was upon me, did so smite them, that I did not hear them say a word against me; and truly when I was Naked in the streets, the Burden was taken off me: that I said in my self, Oh, how easy am I now! it is good to obey the voice of the Lord; so in several places in Wales, did I declare the Message of the Lord.

> (*An Account of Some of the Travels and Sufferings of that Faithful Servant of the Lord, Thomas Briggs*, London, 1685.)

1. Probably Llanrwst.


## DOCUMENT XVII

*This letter was sent to a relation by Col. John Jones, Maesygarnedd, whilst he was in the Tower of London. He was executed as a regicide on 17 October 1660.*

I am very much grieved, to find (by the Note I received from you) such dark and sad Apprehensions upon your Spirit concerning me:

We are in the hands of the Lord, and what he hath appointed for us, will be our portion, and no man can frustrate his holy purpose concerning us; which I question will be found to be in love, what ever appearance it may have to men. My Advice is to you and all that love me, That (in case I be removed from you) you do not, neither in reallity, nor outward garb, mourn for me; but rather rejoyce, that my Portion is in Heaven; and that my Dissolution or Removal out of this earthly Tabernacle, is but in order to my Cloathing with Immortality, and possessing my Eternal Mansion; and to my being for ever with Christ, to behold his glory; And therefore that you do not behave your self, as those that have no hopes but of this life.

Secondly, that you take off your mind from me, and fix it unmovably upon your eternal Relation, the Lord Jesus Christ; in whose glorious and blessed presence, we shall meet ere long, to our Eternal Rejoycing; It is the goodness of the Lord to us, to remove all Creature Comforts from us, that our Souls might have no resting-place to delight in, or to promise them safety; until we return to the Ark of his Testimony, the bosome of his love manifested and exhibited for us, in our blessed Lord Jesus Christ. I write in hast, therefore excuse my abruptness.

Thine in Sincere Love,

Tower, Sept. 19. 1660 John Jones

(*The Speeches and Prayers of . . . Col. John Jones, Octob. 17*, London, 1660.)


## DOCUMENT XVIII

*The manner in which Ellis Rowlands, Puritan minister of Clynnog in Caernarfonshire, was abused and manhandled by some of his parishioners strongly suggests that affection for the Book of Common Prayer remained strong in sheltered, rural areas.*

Articles of misdemeanours exhibited against Beniamin Lloyd and David Evans both of the parish of Clynog fawr in the County of Carnarvon, by Ellis Rowlands Cler. vicar of the said parish, before his Majesties Justices of the peace, sitting in open sessions held for the County of Carnarvon, at the towne of Carnarvon, Jan. 8. 1660[1]. Witnesses of the several misdemeanours. Kadwalader pugh William Roberts. That the said Beniamin lloyd, finding the said Ellis Rowlands to repaire to the parish church of Clynog on the second day of December last did enter into the church and shut the doore against the said ᴸ.lis Rowlands, the said Beniamin uttering these or the like words, ni chei di ddyfod imewn ymma.[1] And the said Beniamin lloyd having the key brought him by the sexton, did come out and locked the doore and went his way thence, though it was the lords day and betweene the houres of eight and ten.

Morgan ap William Probert. Kadwalader pugh. That upon the 16th. day of December last, being ye lords day, the said Beniamin lloyd and David Evans stayed out of church, although the service was begun, and hindered the said Ellis Rowlands from goeing in, though he attempted it divers times: but ye said Beniamin lloyd and David Evans layd hands on the said Ellis Rowlands and kept him from goeing in.

. . . William Thomas William Owen Kadwalader pugh That the said Beniamin lloyd and David Evans did hinder the said Ellis Rowlands upon the said 30th. of December from goeing into the church when the service was begun by another who was admitted in. But when the sd Ellis Rowlands sought to go in at the porch doore (when it was opened for others) they the sd Beniamin lloyd and David Evans did keep him from goeing in. And the said Beniamin did there and then take the said Ellis Rowlands by the shoulder and flung him from one part of the porch to the other. Also when the said Ellis Rowlands sought to go in at the Chancell Beniamin lloyd and David Evans did keep him back and in so doeing the said Beniamin was so fierce as to take hold of the said Ellis by the necke and to teare his coate downe the backe.

William Thomas William Owen Grace ffrancis. That upon the said 30th. day of December, the said David Evans tooke away the bibles of some who were present, and particularly the bible of Grace vch ffrancis and would not restore it but uttered expressions about burning it, saying these or the like words: [ni a fynnwn weled llosci y bibles fydd heb y comon prayer ynddynt][2] or [ni a gawn weled llosci yr holl fibles fydd heb y comon prayer ynddynt][3] and haveing so said he opened and held up the said book saying dymma fo.[4]

(Gwynedd Archives, Caernarfonshire Quarter Sessions Records, 1660.)

1. You shall not come in here.
2. We'll insist on seeing all bibles without a prayer book burnt.
3. We'll see all those bibles without a prayer-book in them burnt.
4. Here it is.

# DOCUMENT XIX

*William Lucy, Bishop of St David's (1660–77), nursed an obsessive hatred of Dissenting preachers and schoolmasters. This petulant letter, written sometime in 1673, was sent to Gilbert Sheldon, Archbishop of Canterbury.*

There has beene constant orders given to the Clergie in this diocesse for instructing children in the Church Catechisme, as well at visitaccions, as upon all other emergent occations. These Instructions have beene followed by ye Clergie for the greatest part, and parents earnestly required to send their children to be Catechised, but doe it not, and their backwardnesse is soe generall yt ye Church censure if used for their correccion would involve whole p[ar]ishes together.

The reason of this neglect I conceive to be partly the generall loosenesse in ye manners of men, and those evill principles formerly instilld during ye late rebellion, for they were governed by Itinerants who looking onely at their owne profit, have soe neglected the meaner Churches, that in very many places they have had noe divine duty performed in them for 10 or 12 yeares together, wth old Leven they are yett soured wth. Besides ye neglect of parents, that wch highly advances the growth of Schisme are ye private schooles, wch in despight of law & coercion are in this part of South Wales erected by seminarys of the dissenting party, and small stipends as 6 or 8 pound per annum (in wch this diocesse seemes to have sufferd more yn any other) allowed to women and other Excommunicated persons to teach Schoole, who instruct the Children in factiuse Catechismes, given them in charge by theire patrons and supporters, These Schooles in my diocesse are erected in Breccon, Carmarthen, Haverford = West, Swanzey, and Cardigan, and severall other places.

Besides these there is at Swanzey one Stephen Hughes a person excommunicated for teaching Schoole wthout license, but lately licensed by his Majesty (as is sayd) to preach at his owne house at Swanzey, and one other place onely. under wch Colour he has intruded himself into severall Churches abt Carmarthen. Countenanced by the leading men of the Country and impropriators whose frownes over awe the poore curates that they feare to deny them . . .

In Carmarthen there is one James Picton[1] a Quaker who teaches Schoole publickly (and stands excommunicated for it) wthout license, for wch the Maior of the towne (required to putt ye Statute in execution) having imprisond him, a writ de homine replegiando[2] was brought, the prison doores broken open and he thus deliverd by the rabble keepes Schoole againe in despight of ye Statute, has 70 or 80 Schollars and an ingeniouse man Schoolmr. of ye Free Schoole has not above 20 or 30. Besides these publick instructers of the youth in this Country there are greate number of teachers, some who pretend to have licenses (but having beene called to shew them will shew none) from his Majesty, of severall perswasions, Quakers especially whose meetings are numerous and the places of their meetings uncertaine.

There is also one Morrice who (as I can learne) has noe license, a teacher errant, who leades a body of 200 or 300 after him in the face of this Country, haveing the last weeke preached twice neere this Town not at all checked or disturbed by the Justices of ye peace.

All these disperse their principles among the people, by papers and bookes instilling their doctrines, preaching & praying in private houses, very sedulouse in promoting theire severall factions.

(Bodleian Library, Tanner MS 146, f.138 r–v.)

1. A Quaker schoolmaster who was dramatically released from Carmarthen prison by daring followers.
2. A writ 'on releasing a man on bail'.

# DOCUMENT XX

*This account of the manner in which Quakers were maltreated by magistrates in Merioneth is written with a fine sense of drama.*

When the Quarter-Sessions came the Constable Brought [them] there, according to his orders. There was six Justices on the Bench, & the Sheriff. Some of them were Men of a Thousand Pounds a Year, & the least two Hundred, — most of them in the Prime of their time. When we came before them, they began to deride, mock & Scoff, and in a Scoffing Manner asking if we did know the Ffydd Gatholig etc., — that is, Catholic faith, etc. Others in a Rage said if we were not Quakers they would make us Quake, — make us their Laughing Stocks, — flinging our hats about. Our friend Evan Ellis said to them that they took more Delight to sit on the Seat of Scorners than on the seat of Justice and Judgment. Then they tendered the Oath to us, which we Refused, then they fined us and upon Default of Payment they Committed us to the gaol. It being late and a long way to the County Prison, we were shut up that Night in a Close Room. When it was Night, by the Light of the Moon the whole Bench, with one accord, Both Sheriff and Justices, save one, came before the door, where we were put in, to make Merry over us & over the witness of God in themselves. Drinking the King's Health, they commanded the Gaoler to open upon us, & sent in their Parasite to force us to drink the King's health. We, lying upon the Ground like Dead bodies, did not mind what they said. They had Liquor which they called *Aqua Vita*. They offered us some of it, & in a Mocking Manner called it the water of Life; [saying] it would flow out of our Bellies if we would drink of it. We Still lay Quiet, answering not a Word. Then they sent the fiddler to Play and sing over us and so Continued Tormenting us almost all night, pouring drink in our faces and committed an Indecency hardly fit to be mentioned. We never moved all this while, for all they could do.

> (John Humphrey, 'A Brief Narrative of the Christian People called
> Quakers at Llwyn Grwill [Llwyngwril] in Merioneth Shire'.
> *Historical Collections relating to Gwynedd*, ed. H.M. Jenkins,
> Philadelphia, 1897, pp.101–2.)

## DOCUMENT XXI

*Although Richard Davies's memoirs were published in relatively tranquil times in 1710, the author's ear for dialogue helps to convey the atmosphere of the years of persecution, and popular attitudes towards the penal code.*

. . . and the Enemy and Adversary of the Growth and Prosperity of Truth in these Parts, stirr'd up an Informer against us, one John David alias Pugh, a Weaver, one who was a Tenant to the Goaler, and we had our Meeting in an Upper Room in our Prison, and the said Informer dwelt below; and once, as he was coming by my Barns, where my Cattle were, he said to some of my Neighbours, These Cattle are all mine: They asked him, how they were his? He said, Richard Davies hath preached three times this Day, and that by the Laws there is £60 on the Preacher for the same. By this, it was noised abroad in the Town, that I was like to be undone; my Neighbours seem'd to be concerned thereat; and one of the Aldermen, that was a Relation of mine, came Chidingly to me, and asked me, Whether I had a mind to Ruine my Wife and Family? Could I not leave my Preaching, when I knew the Laws were so severe against us? I told him, I could not, when the Lord required it of me. I desired him to let the Informer alone, and let him take his course. He said, He would not; But said he, I will tell thee what I will do, I will take him along with me to Severn-side, and whet my knife very sharp, and I will cut off one of the Rogue's Ears; and if ever he informs against thee again, I will cut off the other. I earnestly desired him to let him alone; but he and his Neighbours were so enraged against him, that I was afraid they would have done him some mischief in one place or another.

This informer was a Weaver by Trade, and the Neighbours took their Work away from him, so that his Children went soon after a begging, many of the Town telling them, Their Father had got a new Rich Trade in hand, and that they need not give them any thing. So the poor Children suffer'd very much; but my Wife did not with-hold her Hand of Charity towards them.

(Richard Davies, *An Account of the Convincement, Exercises, Services and Travels of . . . Richard Davies*, London, 1710, pp.169–71.)

# DOCUMENT XXII

*Philip Henry, the Presbyterian minister ejected from his living at Worthenbury, Flintshire, in 1661, agonized long over the implications and likely consequences of the Declaration of Indulgence of 1672.*

16 [March 1672] came forth the K. Declaration for Indulgence, the Church of Engl. establisht, poenal lawes suspended agt. all non-conf. & Recusants, separate places promis'd to bee licens'd, Papists to meet in private houses only; The reason rendred is, the ineffectualnes of rigor for divers yeares & to invite strangers. A thing diversly resented, as men's Interest leades them, the Conformists generally displeas'd at it, the Presb. glad, the Indep. very glad, the Papists triumph.

That the K. hath power herein should seem from his Supremacy in church matters esp. since recogniz'd by late Act agt. Conventicles, however if the lawes hereby suspended as to the non-conf. were, as some say, wicked laws *ab initio*, then to lay ym aside, such think is more clear — The danger is, lest ye allowing of separate places help to overthrow our Parish-order which God hath own'd, & beget divisions & animosityes amongst us which no honest heart but would rather should bee heal'd.

The way were for those in place to admit ye sober non-conf. to preach somet. occasionally in their Pulpits, which would in turn wear off praejudices & mutually strengthen each others hands agt. ye common enemy ye Papist, who will fish best in troubled waters — wee are put hereby to a Trilemma either to turn flat Independents, or to strike in with ye conformists, or to sit down in former silence & sufferings, till the lord shall open a more effectual door . . .

June 3 . . . licenses still freely granted into all pts to all partyes. There are many thoughts of heart about them, what may be in the end thereof, but let us mind our duty & let God alone to order events which are his work & not our's. I have often said, hee that observes the winds shall now sow & hee that regards the clouds shall not reap.

Some think by accepting of yem wee give ye King a power above the lawes, so wee doe above such bad lawes as yt of uniformity. Others think twill end in a severe Tax upon licens'd meetings & persons distinct from others: Others in a Massacre, it being now known where such people may bee mett with, as if they all had but one neck.

(*Diaries and Letters of Philip Henry*, ed. M. H. Lee,
London, 1882, pp.249, 250, 253.)


# DOCUMENT XXIII

*In August and September 1672, Henry Maurice preached to large congregations in unlicensed places in his native Llŷn. His diary (now lost), in Thomas Richards's words, helps 'to enrich, and vivify the dry records of this dark time'.*


September 13 [1672] — I prayed in private this morning, with some enlargement and reviving. I was in a better frame of spirit all this day than I had been several days before. It being the fair-day at Pwllheli, I had occasion to speak with several, which I did with much alacrity, and this was kindness from the Lord in several respects. I prayed after in the evening, having some life and encouragement. So also I prayed in the family, being tempted as the night before. I had some refreshment in discoursing with Hugh Evans, at Richard Thomas's house, this night. I prayed in private after, having little life or refreshment. September 14. — I prayed with my wife, being hard, earnest, and in conflict with my spirit, yet with some satisfaction, having some freedom to plead with God. So I prayed in private after, having atheism, hardness, discouragement, and no sense throughout the duty. I went to see cousin John Williams, being in an inward conflict by the way as I went. We discoursed together very earnestly and seriously about his long silence, and neglecting the Lord's work in that country, insomuch that it drew tears from us both, as I imagined. He told me something of the sense that many in that country had, about my quitting my benefice, that it was done only out of some politic design. He told me also that I must walk very close and upright to recover my credit in that country. He pressed me much to hold forth Christ and his merits as the only justification of a sinner, and advised me to insist much upon that point wherever I went. I prayed in private in the evening, and proceeded to my weekly duty of thanksgiving, being hard, restrained, yet having some sense.

September 15. — Being the Sabbath I prayed with earnestness, yet hard, and without sense for the most part. I went away to the house of Maurice Jones's widow, where I prayed, having a little refreshment; I preached there this day from 1 Peter iv. 18, having little encouragement or enlargement in prayer or preaching. In the afternoon I received a note from my brother, who was at Llanarmon whither he invited me in the afternoon to preach; but coming there, the public place was shut against us by the priest there, so that I preached in the yard, from the same text as in the morning, having much restraint upon my spirit in praying and preaching, yet some of the people were seemingly affected. I rode away thence to Pwllheli this evening, where I prayed a little in private, having encouragement to hope that God would do good to some in that town; I preached there this night from Romans v. 8, and I had much freedom in praying and preaching. Blessed be the Lord.

(Thomas Rees, *History of Protestant Nonconformity in Wales*, 2nd ed., London, 1883, pp.217–18.)

# DOCUMENT XXIV

*Backsliders who brought shame upon the Quaker movement were encouraged to vent their remorse publicly. In this instance, Bridget Berrow, a maid, confessed to committing adultery with Edmond Williams of Haverfordwest.*

Dear friends it is layd upon me from ye Lord to let you understand yt I have sinned against ye Lord God of Heaven, & Earth, & his people in yt I have given you great offences, & greived their tender Consciences, & burthened ye pure seed of God in them by letting my minde run forth toward Edmond Williams not knowing but yt his wife had been dead for I was pswaded in my heart yt she was out of ye body because he sd he had not heard from her in soe long a time as seaven years wch caused me to erre, & hearken to ye subtilty of ye serpent whch wrought in ye missery of iniquity, & begot in me a false birth wch seemed to me to be of God, & ye leadings of his spirit but it was of ye Devill wch is a lyar from ye begining, & ye Spirt of Error wch darkned my understanding, & caused me to follow ye outgoeings of my minde wch was gone a wandring from ye pure light of God in my Conscience; therefore dear friends I doe here wth greife of heart, & shame, & confusion to my face owne my condemnation from ye Lord God & his people & deny, judge & condemne all such disorderly carriage to be of God or ye leading of his spirit but of ye spirit of error & darknes & ye fruits of this world soe from whence it came thither I doe return it wth shame to my face for ever, & woe is me for ever yt I have done this deed against ye Lord my God & ye sheep of his pasture for I have opened ye mouthes of ye wicked, & caused ye Heathen to rejoyce, & brought a reproach upon ye everlasting truth for wch I am a sufferer; oh! woe is me for it, or yt ever I was borne to doe this wickedness; Oh! wt shall I doe where wth shall I appease ye wrath of my God, & make satisfaction to his Saints, & tender lambs for ye Truth is unreprovable who can lay any thing to ye charge of Gods elected ones. Oh! Woe is me for ever for shame & confusion doth cover my face as a vayle, & how shall I appear before ye Lord, & his people for our God is A consumeing fire, & who can dwell wth everlasting burnings but he, yt hath clean hands, & a pure heart; And soe dear friends for your better satisfaction I doe here in ye feare of ye Lord God deny, judge, and condemne and abhorre to have any more to doe wth him then wth another faithfull friend yt walketh spiritually as long as his wife is in ye body; And dear friends in ye fear of ye Lord God I shall desire you to be mindfull of me in your prayers yt my faith faile not for ye Judgmt of ye Lord I must bear untill he hath executed judgmt in ye Earth, and brought it to victory and speaketh peace unto my soule for my tryall is verry great, and A wounded conscience who can bear, & I have not one friend yt is near me.

Given forth ye 7th day of ye 5th month 1668 by Bridget Berrow from ye Common goale in Brecon.

(Glamorgan Record Office, Society of Friends Collection,
D/DSF 1. f.759–60.)

## DOCUMENT XXV

*Richard Davies resisted the temptation to flee to the Promised Land and this letter to William Penn, dated 7 July 1684, is a striking example of his fears for the future of Quakerism in Wales. Note the idiosyncratic style, so different from that of his edited memoirs (Document XXI).*

Deare will its not nether seas nor storms nether danger of siprack keeps me from thee; for I am often with thee in sperit and glad would I be if I in truth be servisable to thee or aney as belongs to thy contrey: I have freely left my self to the disposing of my god in whose fear I stand, by whose councel I desier to be guided. Deare William keep noe place or placis for me to the prediguce of the people for if I com thow shalt see if it pleace god soe to be that we shall Imbrace one another in that contrey that it shall not be for honor or profit: for if those things had bin in my Eye I might have snapt at them when thy love Extend soe largely to mee as I see it doth continue; the feeling and seeing by letters of thy cordial continued kindness to me and mine still oblige mee more and more to love thee thow art noe buble nor mussroom. thow art borne of that stock and seeds that the blessing is unto that we with thee and all the familes that beleves in him coms to be blesed . . .

Dear will the formoest of this was written before and now charls Lloyd John ap Joh and my self being together in Meryonith shire, taking our leave of friends that are boun[d] for thy contrey: seeing maney letters that cam from thence to ther friends here, speack wel of thee, the contrey and Governmt and allsoe that thow hast granted us 4000 acker of land together which is great content to them they be hastning to it as fast as they can, that I think this contrey will be shortly with but few frinds in. som grumbls that soe maney should goe away but it is to little purpose. the god of my life continue thy health and life among them.

(*The Papers of William Penn*, eds. R.S. Dunn and M.M. Dunn, vol. 2, University of Pennsylvania, 1982, p.563.)

## DOCUMENT XXVI

*This winsome account of the many-sided activities of Stephen Hughes (1622–88) 'the Apostle of Carmarthenshire', is based on details provided by James Owen, one of Hughes's most devoted disciples.*

Mr Stephen Hughes. Born in Carmarthen. Sometime after his Ejectment, he married a Pious Woman in Swanzey, whose Portion, Frugality, and Industry, contributed very much to his comfortable Subsistence and Future Usefulness. He was of a publick Spirit, and printed several Welch Books at his own Charge, and among others, the excellent Welch Poems of Mr Rees Pritchard Vicar of Llanymddfri, which contain the Summary of Christian Duties in British Verse. This Book of which he publish'd several Editions, has occasion'd many Hundreds of the Ignorant Welch who delight in Songs, to learn to read their own Language. He assisted in the Correction of the Welch Bible, which Mr Gouge publish'd; and was very Instrumental in getting Subscriptions towards that Impression, which is the best Edition extant of the Old British Bible. He was a plain, Methodical, Affectionate Preacher, and insisted much upon the great and substantial Things of Religion. He seldom preach'd without melting into Tears, which often drew Tears from his Auditors. He affected to preach in the darkest Corners, and in Places where the People had Ignorant Readers, that could not Preach. His Moderation and lively Preaching, recommended him to the Esteem of the sober Part of the Gentry, by whose Connivance he often preach'd in the publick Churches, which were much throng'd by the vast Numbers that came to hear him from the Neighbouring Parishes. He generally preach'd twice on a Lords Day in distant Places; and often rode Eight or Ten Miles, between the Sermons, which much impair'd his Health, and in all probability shortned his Days. He had very great Seals to his Ministry. Great Numbers were reclaim'd from their Sinful and Wicked Ways, and became serious Christians. In most of his Sermons he press'd Faith and Repentance, and exhorted the Illiterate to learn to read their own Language, which great Numbers did, and many of them at forty and fifty Years of Age and above. He would in a very affectionate Address, expose the Sinful and Damnable Nature of Ignorance, recommend the Usefulness, Amiableness, and Necessity of Knowledge, and excite Heads of Families to teach their Children and Servants, and one Neighbour to teach another. He publish'd near a Score of Welch Books, most of them Translations out of English: Such as *The Practise of Piety*, Mr Baxters *Call to the Unconverted*, his *Now or never*,[1] Mr Allein *of Conversion*,[2] *The Plain Man's Pathway to Heaven*, etc. And at the End of most of them he added the Welch Alphabet, to direct People to read. 'Tho he had but a small Income, he was very Charitable; and much given to Hospitality. He was a great Encourager of young Ministers and Christians. He was inoffensive and obliging in his Conversation, and generally belov'd: And his Ministry which was mostly Itinerant, was frequented by vast Numbers of People. This expos'd him to the Censure of the Conservators of the sacred Keys, to whom it was equal, whether they made their Markets by the Sins or by the Piety of the People. These Gentlemen pass'd the Censures of the Church upon him, and not long after deliver'd him to the secular Power, which confin'd him to a close Prison in Carmarden, to the Prejudice of his Health, and Hazard of his Life. But it pleas'd God by a favourable and unexpected Providence to work his Enlargement, by Means of which he recover'd his Health, and Oportunities for farther Service.

(Edmund Calamy, *An Account of the Ministers . . . who were Ejected or Silenced after the Restoration in 1660*, 2 vols., London, 1713, vol. 2, pp.718–19.)

1. Richard Baxter (1615–91), a Presbyterian divine and a prolific author.
2  Joseph Alleine (1634–68), a Puritan author whose book, *An Alarm to the Unconverted*, sold phenomenally well.

# Bibliography

(The place of publication, unless otherwise stated, is London.)

*Printed Sources and Calendars*

**1.** *An Act for the Propagation of the Gospel in Wales, 1650* (Cardiff, 1908).

**2.** Besse, Joseph, *A Collection of the Sufferings of the People called Quakers* (2 vols., 1753). Based on manuscript material in Friends House Library, London.

**3.** Calamy, Edmund, *An Account of the Ministers, Lecturers, Masters and Fellows of Colleges and Schoolmasters, who were Ejected or Silenced after the Restoration in 1660* (2 vols., 1713). An invaluable source for the ejected Puritan ministers. See no. 17.

**4.** Charles, B.G. (ed.), *Calendar of the Records of the Borough of Haverfordwest 1539–1660* (Cardiff, 1967).

**5.** Davies, J.H. (ed.), *Hen Gerddi Gwleidyddol: 1558–1660* (Caerdydd, 1901). Includes a number of anti-Puritan songs.

**6.** Davies, Richard, *An Account of the Convincement, Exercises, Services, and Travels of . . . Richard Davies 1710* (Gregynog, 1928). Published posthumously, this autobiography reveals a real gift for narrative.

**7.** Firth, C.H. and Rait, R.S. (eds.), *Acts and Ordinances of the Interregnum, 1642–1660* (3 vols., 1911).

**8.** Fortescue, G.K. (ed.), *British Museum Catalogue of the Pamphlets, Books, Newspapers, and Manuscripts relating to the Civil War, the Commonwealth, and Restoration collected by George Thomason, 1640–1661* (2 vols., 1908). An indispensable guide.

**9.** Gibbard, Noel, *Elusen i'r Enaid: Arweiniad i Weithiau'r Piwritaniaid Cymreig, 1630–1689* (Pen-y-bont ar Ogwr, 1979). A useful selection of Puritan documents.

**10.** Griffith, Alexander, *Strena Vavasoriensis 1654* (Cardiff, 1915).

**11.** Jones, E.D., 'Llyfr Eglwys Mynydd Bach', *Y Cofiadur*, 17 (1947).

**12.** Jones, J.M. (ed.), 'Llyfr Eglwys y Cilgwyn', *Y Cofiadur*, 1 (1923).

**13.** Lee, M.H. (ed.), *Diaries and Letters of Philip Henry* (1882). A wonderful collection. Henry's original diaries were written with a crowquill in popular almanacs.

**14.** Lewis, Henry (ed.), *Hen Gyflwyniadau* (Caerdydd, 1948).

**15.** Llwyd, Morgan, *Gweithiau Morgan Llwyd o Wynedd*, ed. J.H. Davies and T.E. Ellis (2 vols., Bangor, 1899; London, 1908). Vol. III is forthcoming (Cardiff, 1992), ed. J. Graham Jones and Goronwy Wyn Owen. The works of the most intellectually gifted and intriguing Welsh Puritan.

**16.** Martin, L.C. (ed.), *The Works of Henry Vaughan* (2nd ed., Oxford, 1957). Literature which expresses the Anglican viewpoint with poignancy and passion. See no.26.

**17.** Matthews, A.G. (ed.), *Calamy Revised* (Oxford, 1934).

**18.** Matthews, A.G. (ed.), *John Walker Revised* (Oxford, 1948).

**19.** Miles, John, *An Antidote against the Infection of the Times 1656*, ed. T. Shankland (Cardiff, 1904).

**20.** Morgan, Merfyn (ed.), *Gweithiau Oliver Thomas ac Evan Roberts* (Caerdydd, 1981).

**21.** Nickalls, J.L. (ed.), *The Journal of George Fox* (Cambridge, 1952). Includes an account of the famous tour of Wales in 1657.

**22.** Owens, B.G., 'Llawysgrifau Joshua Thomas, Llanllieni', *Trafodion Cymdeithas Hanes Bedyddwyr Cymru* (1969).

**23.** Phillips, J. Roland, *Memoirs of the Civil War in Wales and the Marches 1642–1649* (2 vols., 1874).

**24.** Rees, Thomas, *History of Protestant Nonconformity in Wales* (2nd ed., 1883). Contains much valuable material not available elsewhere, but marred by unsubstantiated judgements and a surfeit of 'seraphic' adjectives.

**25.** Richards, Thomas, 'The Religious Census of 1676', *Trans. Hon. Soc. Cymmrodorion*, Supplement (1925–6). Should be read in conjunction with no.32.

**26.** Rudrum, Alan (ed.), *Henry Vaughan: The Complete Poems* (repr. ed., Harmondsworth, 1983).

**27.** Thomas, Joshua, *Hanes y Bedyddwyr* (Carmarthen, 1778). Heavily anecdotal but well-informed and sympathetic.

**28.** Underhill, E.B. (ed.), *The Records of a Church of Christ Meeting at Broadmead, Bristol* (1847). Contains an account by Henry Maurice of the number of Congregationalist churches in Wales in 1675.

**29.** Walker, John, *An Attempt towards recovering an Account of the Numbers and Sufferings of the Clergy of the Church of England* (1714). The Anglican reply to Calamy. See no. 18.

**30.** Watkyns, Rowland, *Flamma Sine Fumo* [*1662*], ed. Paul C. Davies (Cardiff, 1968).

**31.** White, B.R. (ed.), *Association Records of the Particular Baptists of England, Wales and Ireland to 1660* (3 vols., 1971–4).

**32.** Whiteman, Anne (ed.), *The Compton Census of 1676: A Critical Edition* (1986). A meticulous analysis.

**33.** Williams, G.J., 'Cerddi i Biwritaniaid Gwent a Morgannwg', *Llên Cymru*, 3 (1954–5).

## The Historiography of Dissent

**34.** Evans, Beriah Gwynfe, *Diwygwyr Cymru* (Caernarfon, 1900). Mischievous, provocative and unreliable.

**35.** Hughes, G.H. (ed.), *Gweithiau William Williams Pantycelyn, Cyfrol II, Rhyddiaith* (Caerdydd, 1967). One-dimensional history, but marvellously vivid prose.

**36.** Hughes, John, *Methodistiaeth Cymru* (3 vols., Wrecsam, 1851–6). Ponderous, uncritical, a blow-by-blow narrative.

**37.** Jenkins, R.T., 'Er Cof: Thomas Richards (1878–1962)', *Trafodion Cymdeithas Hanes Bedyddwyr Cymru* (1963).

**38.** Johnes, A.J., *An Essay on the Causes which have produced Dissent from the Established Church in the Principality of Wales* (1831). Widely employed in its day for political purposes.

**39.** Jones, J. Morgan and William Morgan, *Y Tadau Methodistaidd* (2 vols., Abertawe, 1895–7). A fulsome paean to the Methodist fathers.

**40.** Jones, Robert, *Drych yr Amseroedd 1820*, ed. G.M. Ashton (Caerdydd, 1958). Stylish but anecdotal and impressionistic.

**41.** Morgan, D. Densil, 'Athrawiaeth Hanes Joshua Thomas', *Trafodion Cymdeithas Hanes Bedyddwyr Cymru* (1986).

**42.** Owens, B.G., 'Joshua Thomas, hanesydd y Bedyddwyr', *Y Llenor*, 27 (1948).

**43.** Parry, Thomas, 'Thomas Richards 1878–1962', *Trafodion Cymdeithas Hanes Bedyddwyr Cymru* (1979). A fine tribute to a master craftsman.

**44.** Richards, Thomas, 'Thomas Shankland', *Trafodion Cymdeithas Hanes Bedyddwyr Cymru* (1926).

**45.** Shankland, Thomas, '"Diwygwyr Cymru"(Beriah Gwynfe Evans)', *Seren Gomer*, 21–5 (1900–4).

**46.** Williams, W.G., 'A critical study of the writings of Robert Jones, Rhoslan', (unpubl. University of Liverpool M.A. thesis, 1937).

## *The English Background*

**47.** Acheson, R.J., *Radical Puritans in England, 1550–1660* (1990).

**48.** Capp, B.S., *The Fifth Monarchy Men* (1972). Includes valuable material on Llwyd and Powell.

**49.** Cragg, G.R., *Puritanism in the Period of the Great Persecution, 1660–88* (Cambridge, 1957).

**50.** Dow, F.D., *Radicalism in the English Revolution 1640–1660* (1985). An admirable introduction to radical sectarianism.

**51.** Hill, Christopher, *The World Turned Upside Down* (1975). A challenging work; especially refreshing on people like Erbery and the revolutionary wing of popular radicalism.

**52.** McGregor, J. and Reay, B. (eds.), *Radical Religion in the English Revolution* (Oxford, 1984).

**53.** Nuttall, G.F., *The Holy Spirit in Puritan Faith and Experience* (Oxford, 1946). The first in a series of judicious studies on the Puritan tradition by an erudite scholar.

**54.** Nuttall, G.F., *The Puritan Spirit* (1967).

**55.** Nuttall, G.F., *Visible Saints* (Oxford, 1957).

**56.** Reay, Barry, *The Quakers and the English Revolution* (1985). A fresh reappraisal of the Quakers.

**57.** Watts, Michael R., *The Dissenters from the Reformation to the French Revolution* (Oxford, 1978). The best introduction and required reading for all students of the subject.

**58.** White, B.R., *The English Baptists in the Seventeenth Century* (1983).

*General Works on Wales*

**59.** Davies, John, *Hanes Cymru* (1990).

**60.** Dodd, A.H., 'The pattern of politics in Stuart Wales', *Trans. Hon. Soc. Cymmrodorion* (1948).

**61.** Dodd, A.H., *Studies in Stuart Wales* (2nd ed., Cardiff, 1971). A series of lucid essays written by a master of the subject.

**62.** Evans, E.D., *A History of Wales, 1660–1815* (Cardiff, 1976).

**63.** Jenkins, Geraint H., *The Foundations of Modern Wales: Wales, 1642–1780* (Oxford and Cardiff, 1987). The most up-to-date general synthesis.

**64.** Jenkins, Geraint H., *Hanes Cymru yn y Cyfnod Modern Cynnar, 1530–1760* (Caerdydd, 1983).

**65.** Thomas, Hugh, *A History of Wales, 1485–1660* (Cardiff, 1972).

**66.** Thomas, W.S.K., *Stuart Wales* (Llandysul, 1988).

**67.** Walker, David (ed.), *A History of the Church in Wales* (Penarth, 1976).

**68.** Williams, Glanmor, *Grym Tafodau Tân* (Llandysul, 1984). A stimulating collection of essays. See nos. 69, 70.

**69.** Williams, Glanmor, *Religion, Language and Nationality in Wales* (Cardiff, 1979).

**70.** Williams, Glanmor, *Welsh Reformation Essays* (Cardiff, 1967).

*Puritans and Separatists*

**71.** Dodd, A.H., 'New England influences in early Welsh Puritanism', *Bulletin of the Board of Celtic Studies*, 16 (1954).

**72.** Dodd, A.H., 'A Remonstrance from Wales, 1655', *Bulletin of the Board of Celtic Studies*, 17 (1958).

**73.** Evans, E. Lewis, *Morgan Llwyd* (Lerpwl, 1931).

**74.** Gibbard, Noel, *Walter Cradock: 'A New Testament Saint'* (Bridgend, 1977).

**75.** Gruffydd, R.G., *'In that Gentile Country': The Beginnings of Puritan Nonconformity in Wales* (Bridgend, 1976). A helpful introduction to pre-Propagation Puritanism.

**76.** Gruffydd, R.G., 'William Wroth a chychwyniadau Anghydffurfiaeth yng Nghymru', *Ysgrifau Diwinyddol* (Pen-y-bont ar Ogwr, 1988).

**77.** Hill, Christopher, 'Propagating the Gospel', in H.E. Bell and R.L. Ollard (eds.), *Historical Essays, 1600–1750* (1963). The best introduction to the Propagation period.

**78.** Hill, Christopher, 'Puritans and the "Dark Corners of the Land"', *Trans. Royal Historical Soc.*, 13 (1963).

**79.** James, B.Ll., 'The evolution of a radical: the life and career of William Erbery (1604–54)', *Journal of Welsh Ecclesiastical History*, 3 (1986).

**80.** James, E. Wyn (ed.), *Cwmwl o Dystion* (Abertawe, 1977).

**81.** Johnson, A.M., 'Wales during the Commonwealth and Protectorate', in D. Pennington and K. Thomas (eds.), *Puritans and Revolutionaries* (Oxford, 1978).

**82.** Jones, J. Gwynfor, 'Agweddau ar dwf Piwritaniaeth yn Sir Gaernarfon: tystiolaeth cofnodion llywodraeth leol', *Y Traethodydd*, 141 (1986).

**83.** Jones, J. Gwynfor, 'Caernarvonshire administration: the activities of the justices of the peace, 1603–1660', *Welsh History Review*, 5 (1970–1).

**84.** Jones, J. Gwynfor, 'Piwritaniaeth gynnar yng Nghymru a sefydlu Eglwys Llanfaches, 1639', *Y Cofiadur*, 55 (1990).

**85.** Jones, J.M., 'Walter Cradock a'i gyfoeswyr', *Y Cofiadur*, 15 (1938).

**86.** Jones, John W. (ed.), *Coffa Morgan Llwyd* (Llandysul, 1952).

**87.** Jones, R. Tudur, 'The healing herb and the rose of love: the piety of two Welsh puritans', in R. Buick Knox (ed.), *Reformation, Conformity and Dissent* (1977).

**88.** Jones, R. Tudur, 'The life, work and thought of Vavasor Powell (1617–70)' (unpubl. University of Oxford D.Phil. thesis, 1947).

**89.** Jones, R. Tudur, 'Pulpud Llanfaches: efengyl Walter Cradoc', *Y Cofiadur*, 55 (1990).

**90.** Jones, R. Tudur, *Vavasor Powell* (Abertawe, 1971). An excellent biography.

**91.** Jones, R. Tudur, *Vavasor Powell* (Leominster, 1975). A brief summary in English of no.90.

**92.** Nuttall, G.F., *The Welsh Saints, 1640–1660* (Cardiff, 1957).

**93.** Owen, G.W., 'Astudiaeth hanesyddol a beirniadol o weithiau Morgan Llwyd o Wynedd (1619–1659)', (unpubl. University of Wales Ph.D. thesis, 1982).

**94.** Richards, Thomas, *Cymru a'r Uchel Gomisiwn, 1633–40* (Lerpwl, 1930).

**95.** Richards, Thomas, 'Eglwys Llanfaches', *Trans. Hon. Soc. Cymmrodorion* (1941).

**96.** Richards, Thomas, 'Flintshire and the Puritan movement', *Journal Flintshire Hist. Soc.*, 12–14 (1951–4).

**97.** Richards, Thomas, *A History of the Puritan Movement in Wales, 1639–53* (1920). A pioneering study, but forbiddingly detailed.

**98.** Richards, Thomas, 'The Puritan movement in Anglesey: a re-assessment', *Trans. Anglesey Antiq. Soc.* (1954).

**99.** Roberts, Stephen, 'Godliness and government in Glamorgan, 1647–1660', in Colin Jones et al. (eds.), *Politics and People in Revolutionary England* (Oxford, 1986). Offers fresh insights on the links between Puritanism and profiteering.

**100.** Roberts, Stephen, 'Welsh Puritanism in the Interregnum', *History Today* (March 1991).

**101.** Thomas, M. Wynn, *Morgan Llwyd* (Cardiff, 1984). A subtle and perceptive essay.

**102.** Thomas, M. Wynn, 'Morgan Llwyd y Piwritan', in G.H. Jenkins (ed.), *Cof Cenedl III* (Llandysul, 1988).

**103.** Veysey, A.G., 'Colonel Philip Jones, 1618–74', *Trans. Hon. Soc. Cymmrodorion* (1966).

**104.** Watts, Trevor, 'William Wroth (1570–1641). Father of Welsh Nonconformity', *Congregational History Magazine*, II (1989).

**105.** Watts, Trevor, 'William Wroth (1570–1641). Piwritan ac Apostol Cymru', *Y Cofiadur*, 44 (1979).

**106.** Williams, Glanmor, 'The earliest Nonconformists in Merthyr Tydfil', *Merthyr Historian*, 1 (1976).

**107.** Williams, J. Gwynn, 'Rhai agweddau ar y gymdeithas Gymreig yn yr ail ganrif ar bymtheg', *Efrydiau Athronyddol*, 30 (1968).

## Dissenters and the Penal Code

**108.** Davies, Pennar, 'Episodes in the history of Brecknockshire Dissent', *Brycheiniog*, 3 (1957).

**109.** Greaves, R.L., *Deliver Us from Evil: The Radical Underground in Britain, 1660–1663* (Oxford, 1986).

**110.** Greaves, R.L., *Enemies Under His Feet: Radicals and Nonconformists in Britain, 1664–1677* (Stanford, 1990).

**111.** Jenkins, Philip, '"The Old Leaven": the Welsh Roundheads after 1660', *The Historical Journal*, 24 (1981).

**112.** Jones, E.D., 'Ymneilltuaeth gynnar yng Ngheredigion', *Ceredigion*, 4 (1960–3).

**113.** Jones, Francis, 'Disaffection and Dissent in Pembrokeshire', *Trans. Hon. Soc. Cymmrodorion* (1946–7).

**114.** Jones, R. Tudur, 'Eglwys Loegr a'r Saint, 1660–1688', *Diwinyddiaeth*, 14 (1963).

**115.** Jones, R. Tudur, 'Religion in post-Restoration Brecknockshire, 1660–1688', *Brycheiniog*, 8 (1962).

**116.** Jones, R. Tudur and Owens, B.G., 'Anghydffurfwyr Cymru, 1660–1662', *Y Cofiadur*, 32 (1962). Lists, with biographical details, ejected Puritan ministers, 1660–2.

**117.** Morgan, W.T., 'The prosecution of Nonconformists in the consistory courts of St David's, 1661–88', *Journal Hist. Soc. Church* *in Wales*, 12 (1962). A patient and careful study, based on primary sources.

**118.** Richards, Thomas, 'Declarasiwn 1687: tipyn o'i hanes a barn Cymru am dano', *Trafodion Cymdeithas Hanes Bedyddwyr Cymru* (1924).

**119.** Richards, Thomas, *Religious Developments in Wales (1654–1662)* (1923). Packed with remorseless detail.

**120.** Richards, Thomas, *Wales under the Indulgence (1672–1675)* (1928).

**121.** Richards, Thomas, *Wales under the Penal Code 1662–1687* (1925).

**122.** Richards, Thomas, *Piwritaniaeth a Pholitics (1689–1719)* (Wrecsam, 1927).

## The Congregationalists

**123.** Davies, Idris, 'Dyddiau cynnar Annibyniaeth ym Mrycheiniog a Maesyfed', *Y Cofiadur*, 16 (1946).

**124.** *Hanes ac Egwyddorion Annibynwyr Cymru* (Abertawe, 1939).

**125.** Hugh, R.L., 'Annibyniaeth yng Ngorllewin Morgannwg', *Y Cofiadur*, 18 (1948).

**126.** Jones, Iorwerth (ed.), *Yr Annibynwyr Cymraeg: Ddoe, Heddiw ac Yfory* (Abertawe, 1989).

**127.** Jones, R. Tudur, *Hanes Annibynwyr Cymru* (Swansea, 1966). The definitive study of the Welsh Congregationalists.

**128.** Jones, R. Tudur, 'Trefniadaeth ryngeglwysig yr Annibynwyr', *Y Cofiadur*, 21 (1951).

**129.** Owen, J. Dyfnallt, 'Camre cyntaf Anghydffurfiaeth ac Annibyniaeth yn Sir Gaerfyrddin: yr hanner can mlynedd cyntaf, 1660–1710', *Y Cofiadur*, 13 (1936).

**130.** Peate, I.C., 'Lle'r ffiniau yn natblygiad Annibyniaeth yng Nghymru', *Y Cofiadur*, 7 (1929).

**131.** Rees, Thomas, and Thomas, John (eds.), *Hanes Eglwysi Annibynol Cymru* (4 vols., Lerpwl, 1871–5). A mine of information, but badly organized and hardly dispassionate.

**132.** Richards, Thomas, 'Henry Maurice: Piwritan ac Annibynnwr', *Y Cofiadur*, 5–6 (1928).

## The Baptists

**133.** Absalom, J. and Williams, E. Llwyd, *Rhamant Rhydwilym* (Llandysul, 1939).

**134.** Bassett, T.M., *The Welsh Baptists* (Swansea, 1977); published in Welsh as *Bedyddwyr Cymru* (Abertawe, 1977). A thorough and reliable digest of current knowledge.

**135.** James, J. Spinther, *Hanes y Bedyddwyr yng Nghymru* (4 vols., Caerfyrddin, 1896–1907). Old-fashioned and repetitive.

**136.** Jenkins, Geraint H., 'James Owen versus Benjamin Keach: a controversy over infant baptism', *National Library of Wales Journal*, 19 (1975–6).

**137.** John, Mansel (ed.), *Welsh Baptist Studies* (Llandysul, 1976).

**138.** Matthews, D. Hugh, 'Bedyddwyr Maesyfed yn yr 17eg ganrif: gwers mewn goddefgarwch', *Trafodion Cymdeithas Hanes Bedyddwyr Cymru* (1986).

**139.** Matthews, D. Hugh, 'Cyffes ffydd Rhydwilym', *Trafodion Cymdeithas Hanes Bedyddwyr Cymru* (1979).

**140.** Owens, B.G., 'Trichanmlwyddiant Rhydwilym', *Trafodion Cymdeithas Hanes Bedyddwyr Cymru* (1968).

**141.** Phillips, D. Rhys, 'Cefndir hanes Eglwys Ilston, 1649–60', *Trafodion Cymdeithas Hanes Bedyddwyr Cymru* (1928).

**142.** Richards, Thomas, 'Eglwys Rhydwilym', *Trafodion Cymdeithas Hanes Bedyddwyr Cymru* (1938).

**143.** Rhys, W.J., *Penodau yn Hanes y Bedyddwyr Cymreig* (Abertawe, 1949).

**144.** White, B.R., 'The organization of the Particular Baptists, 1644–1660', *Journal of Ecclesiastical History*, 17 (1966).

## The Quakers

**145.** Bebb, W.A., 'John ap John. Apostol y Crynwyr yng Nghymru', *Cymru*, 61 (1921).

146. Browning, C.H., *Welsh Settlement of Pennsylvania* (Philadelphia, 1912).

147. Dodd, A.H., 'The background of the Welsh Quaker migration to Pennsylvania', *Journal Merioneth Hist. and Record Soc.*, III (1958).

148. Glenn, T.A., *Welsh Founders of Pennsylvania* (2 vols., Oxford, 1911–13).

149. Jenkins, Geraint H., 'The early peace testimony in Wales', *Llafur*, IV (1985).

150. Jenkins, Geraint H., 'The Friends of Montgomeryshire in the heroic age', *Montgomeryshire Collections*, 76 (1988).

151. Jenkins, Geraint H., 'From Ysgeifiog to Pennsylvania: the rise of Thomas Wynne, Quaker barber-surgeon', *Flintshire Historical Society Journal*, 28 (1977–8).

152. Jenkins, Geraint H., 'Llythyr olaf Thomas Wynne o Gaerwys: "A Farewell of endeared love to ould England and Wales, 1686"', *Bulletin of the Board of Celtic Studies*, 29 (1982).

153. Morris, E.R., 'Quakerism in West Montgomeryshire', *Montgomeryshire Collections*, 56 (1959–60).

154. Norris, W.G., *John ap John and Early Records of Friends in Wales* (1907).

155. Rees, T. Mardy, *A History of the Quakers in Wales* (Carmarthen, 1925). A rambling study, laced with tedious lists and digressions.

156. Williams, J. Gwynn, 'The Quakers of Merioneth during the seventeenth century', *Journal Merioneth Hist. and Record Soc.*, 8 (1978–9). A richly enjoyable study and a model of its kind.

157. Williams, M. Fay, 'Glamorgan Quakers 1654–1900', *Morgannwg*, 5 (1961).

158. Williams, M. Fay, 'The Society of Friends in Glamorgan, 1654–1900' (unpubl. University of Wales MA thesis, 1950).

## Literature and Education

159. Bevan, Hugh, *Morgan Llwyd y Llenor* (Caerdydd, 1954).

160. Edwards, Charles, *Y Ffydd Ddi-ffvant*, ed. G.J. Williams (Caerdydd, 1936). An edition of one of the most compelling original works by a Welsh Dissenter.

**161.** Hughes, G.H., 'Cefndir meddwl yr ail ganrif ar bymtheg', *Efrydiau Athronyddol*, 18 (1955).

**162.** Jenkins, Geraint H., *Cadw Tŷ Mewn Cwmwl Tystion: Ysgrifau Hanesyddol ar Grefydd a Diwylliant* (Llandysul, 1990). Probes the links between religion and culture.

**163.** Jenkins, Geraint H., *Literature, Religion and Society in Wales, 1660–1730* (Cardiff, 1978). A detailed study of patrons, books and readers.

**164.** Jenkins, Geraint H., 'Llenyddiaeth, crefydd a'r gymdeithas yng Nghymru, 1660–1730', *Efrydiau Athronyddol*, 41 (1978).

**165.** Jenkins, Geraint H., 'Quaker and Anti-Quaker literature in Welsh from the Restoration to Methodism', *Welsh History Review*, 7 (1976).

**166.** Jones, M.G., *The Charity School Movement* (Cambridge, 1938). A pioneering study which has worn unusually well.

**167.** Jones, M.G. (ed.), 'Two accounts of the Welsh Trust, 1675 and 1678', *Bulletin of the Board of Celtic Studies*, 9 (1937).

**168.** Morgan, D. Llwyd, 'A critical study of the works of Charles Edwards (1628–91?)' (unpubl. University of Oxford D.Phil. thesis, 1967).

**169.** Nuttall, G.F., 'The correspondence of John Lewis, Glasgrug, with Richard Baxter and with Dr John Ellis, Dolgellau', *Journal Merioneth Hist. and Record Soc.*, 2 (1953–6).

**170.** Owen, Geraint D., *Ysgolion a Cholegau'r Annibynwyr* (Llandysul, 1939).

**171.** Roberts, H.P., 'Nonconformist academies in Wales (1662–1862)', *Trans. Hon. Soc. Cymmrodorion* (1928–9).

**172.** Rudrum, Alan, *Henry Vaughan* (Cardiff, 1981).

**173.** Vincent, W.A.L., *The State and School Education, 1640–60, in England and Wales* (1950).

**174.** Williams, G.J., 'Stephen Hughes a'i gyfnod', *Y Cofiadur*, 4 (1926).

**175.** Williams, Jac L. and G.R. Hughes (eds.), *The History of Education in Wales* (Swansea, 1978).

## Local Background Studies

**176.** Bowen, E.G., 'The Teifi Valley as a religious frontier', *Ceredigion*, 7 (1972).

**177.** Carter, Harold, *The Towns of Wales* (Cardiff, 1965).

**178.** Dodd, A.H., *A History of Caernarvonshire, 1284–1900* (Caernarfonshire Hist. Soc., 1968).

**179.** Dodd, A.H. (ed.), *A History of Wrexham* (Wrexham, 1957).

**180.** Howells, Brian (ed.), *Pembrokeshire County History vol. III. Early Modern Pembrokeshire, 1536–1815* (Haverfordwest, 1987).

**181.** John, E. Stanley, 'Braslun o ddechreuadau Ymneilltuaeth yn Abertawe', *Y Cofiadur*, 48 (1983).

**182.** Jones, O.W. and Walker, D. (eds.), *Links with the Past: Swansea and Brecon Historical Essays* (Llandybïe, 1974).

**183.** Lloyd, J.E. (ed.), *A History of Carmarthenshire* (vol.2, Cardiff, 1939).

**184.** Palmer, A.N., *A History of the Older Nonconformity of Wrexham* (Wrexham, [1888]).

**185.** Thomas, W.S.K., *The History of Swansea* (Llandysul, 1990).

**186.** Williams, Glanmor (ed.), *Early Modern Glamorgan: Glamorgan County History*, vol. 4 (Cardiff, 1974).

**187.** Williams, Glanmor (ed.), *Swansea: An Illustrated History* (Swansea, 1990).

# Index